The Supreme Court and the News Media

The Supreme Court
and
the News Media

DAVID L. GREY

NORTHWESTERN UNIVERSITY PRESS
Evanston   1968

Material from the following works has been quoted with permission of the publishers: "Journalism and the Prayer Decision," by William A. Hachten. *Columbia Journalism Review*, Fall, 1962:4–9; Winter, 1963:54. *The Supreme Court in Modern Role* by Carl B. Swisher. New York: New York University Press, 1958 and 1965.

David L. Grey is Assistant Professor of Communication
at Stanford University, Stanford, California.

For Lou, Eric, and Mark

Acknowledgments

AN EXPRESSION OF DEBT is owed to the many who were willing to share their thoughts and time as participants in or close observers of this problem in communication. Besides those willing to respond to questions in personal interviews or by mail, special appreciation must be expressed to J. Edward Gerald, Robert L. Jones, and those at the Graduate School of the University of Minnesota who in their own special ways offered encouragement and aid during those vital early stages of research; to the Brookings Institution, Washington, D.C., for providing research facilities for me as a Guest Scholar; and to William A. Hachten of the University of Wisconsin, Eugene J. Webb of Northwestern University, and Chilton R. Bush and William L. Rivers of Stanford University for sharing their research materials and ideas on this topic.

The burdens of execution are, of course, mine alone. It is only hoped that the critical approach used here will be accepted in the spirit intended—as a constructive analysis of two of modern society's most complex, controversial, and relevant democratic institutions.

DAVID L. GREY
Stanford, California
October 17, 1967

Contents

The Supreme Court and the News Media

I

A Problem in Communication

AT ABOUT 10:40 A.M. on Monday, April 5, 1965, Chief Justice Earl Warren paused momentarily after announcing the orders of the Court. From the raised bench in the high-ceilinged courtroom of the marbled Supreme Court Building, he glanced down and across the room to the rows of seats filled with lawyers, interested spectators, and curious tourists. The Chief Justice then picked up a single sheet of paper containing a short, typed announcement. In a formal but rather matter-of-fact tone, he read aloud:

> The Court announces that commencing the week of April 26, 1965, it will no longer adhere to the practice of reporting its decisions only at Monday sessions, and that in the future they will be reported as they become ready for decision at any session of the Court. As in the past, no announcement of decisions to be reported will be made prior to their rendition in open Court.

This single episode in Court history—the ending of the tradition of "Decision Monday"—dramatically illustrates with broad strokes part of a sustaining problem faced by the highest tribunal in the country and the news media covering it: the difficulty of communicating often complex decisions to both legal and lay publics. The tradition of Monday-only decision days was dropped in an effort to alter the spasmodic flood of written opinions—sometimes five, ten, or even fifteen decisions—which might be released to the news media within only an hour or two. Although now only several or half a dozen opinions usually flow from the justices on any one decision day, much of the communication problem has not been resolved. The Court still speaks on complex issues—often at great length and with multiple concurring and dissenting opinions—and then remains silent; the press still is left with the task of trying to interpret such floods of legal words within minutes or only a few hours. As observed by one law professor:

> The difficulties in reporting the significance and facts of United States Supreme Court opinions in the mass media have long been recognized. The problems result from several special circumstances. The Supreme Court unlike other agencies of government is unable, by its very nature, to comment upon its own product or to engage in public relations activities in its own behalf. Its opinions must speak for themselves, even though on occasion these may be very technical and easily misunderstood by inexpert audiences.
>
> The second major difficulty arises from the variety of types of cases and the technicality of many of the fields covered. No one individual, even a lawyer, can easily understand the significance of many of the cases decided by the United States Supreme Court.
>
> Finally . . . although dates of opinion days may be known in advance, the number and identity of cases decided is not known ahead of time. Toward the end of a term, in early June . . . many . . . cases may appear in one day. It becomes extremely difficult, in the short time available, to comprehend and report all the decisions. It is also extremely difficult for editorial writers to treat these important matters with an intelligent sense of criticism or praise.[1]

This book thus attempts to analyze one difficult situation of interaction between government and press. The purpose is to dissect the complex communication factors involved and, where possible, to trace their seeming effects on news information and meaning transmitted about the Court. At the same time, this study attempts to probe and raise questions about the possible significance of these findings for other fields of news communication.

1. This capsuled discussion of the problem appeared as a Feb. 12, 1965, letter from Law Professor Henry G. Manne to *Editor & Publisher* magazine. The letter was designed to explain a project by the Association of American Law Schools (AALS) to write background analyses of Supreme Court cases for use by the news media. This AALS venture, aimed to help the press understand Court decisions, is itself discussed later in this book as a significant problem-solving effort.

CONCERN ABOUT PRESS PERFORMANCE IN A DEMOCRACY

There is perhaps no area of news more inaccurately reported factually, on the whole, though with some notable exceptions, than legal news.

Some part of this is due to carelessness, often induced by the haste with which news is gathered and published, a smaller portion to bias or more blameworthy causes. But a great deal of it must be attributed, in candor, to ignorance which frequently is not at all blameworthy. For newspapers are conducted by men who are laymen to the law. With too rare exceptions their capacity for misunderstanding the significance of legal events and procedures, not to speak of opinions, is great. But this is neither remarkable nor peculiar to newsmen. For the law, as lawyers best know, is full of perplexities.

This indictment of the press by Justice Wiley B. Rutledge in the 1946 case, *Pennekamp* v. *Florida*, does not prove guilt of the press; but it does offer impressive testimony that a real news communication problem has existed. It is ironic that, while news coverage of the Court and the law has improved in some ways in recent years, such criticism has, if anything, increased.[2] The concern most often expressed is that today's society is becoming increasingly complex (as is reflected in the law) but that the press is failing to handle such complexity adequately.

At this point it is necessary to make explicit several of the philosophical concerns underlying such attacks on press performance. Perhaps primary is the belief that the press serves as one essential link between the governors and the governed—between the often remote elected or appointed official in a democracy and the citizens he represents. The press helps to connect the government with public opinion and through this role helps in the creation and transmission of public attitudes, both unified and splintered.

Contrary to what some argue, the Supreme Court does not operate in a vacuum nor as an organism unrelated to conditions and pressures around it. In fact, probably the most important single factor at work on the Court is this amorphous power of public reaction. The

2. A quick tally of published criticism of Court news coverage shows that the bulk of the commentary has been written since 1962—obviously triggered primarily by the controversial New York Regents school prayer case (*Engel* v. *Vitale*). For documentation supporting the paradoxical view that coverage in recent years in some ways has also vastly improved, see especially: Alan F. Westin, "The Business of the Court," *New York Times Book Review*, March 7, 1965, p. 3.

Court decides the law and in this role is a leader of public opinion; but, clearly, the Court is also a follower of public opinion, responding at times in a variety of ways to changing society.

A Supreme Court justice is under less pressure than the elected official to follow public opinion. Still, he cannot overlook objections to his policy preferences and do whatever he wishes to mold society. Clearly, as legal scholars have noted, public concurrence sets an "outer boundary" for his judicial decisions. In addition, the ease or difficulty of law enforcement varies with the extent to which the public regards a Court decision as right.

The obvious question is then: How can the public make up its mind as to whether a law is good or bad unless it knows what the law is? This question does not assume that everyone should, or will ever, be fully informed. It does assume that for public opinion to interact with the Court there should be minimum levels of understanding by the public or at least by policy leaders and those in positions of responsibility.

Yet in this communications setting, according to *The Guardian* correspondent Max Freedman, the work of the Court is "often a puzzle," especially to members of the press. Freedman wrote in 1956: "It seems simply inconceivable . . . that the average American editor would ever dare to write on a debate in Congress or a decision by the President with the meager preparation which he often manifests in evaluating the judgments of the Supreme Court." His conclusion: "I must declare my conviction that the Supreme Court is the worst reported and worst judged institution in the American system of government." [3]

Or, as former Court newsman James E. Clayton of the *Washington Post* observed more recently: "It is certainly true that the American press does not do a very good job of reporting to the public what the Supreme Court does. All too many news executives think the Court can be adequately covered simply by sending a reporter up . . . to collect the opinions." [4]

Concern here is expressed for more than just problems of distor-

3. "Worst Reported Institution," *Nieman Reports*, 10(April, 1956): 2.
4. Edward Douglass White Lecture Series, Georgetown University Law Center, Nov. 18, 1964.

tion, bias, or error in fact. The criticism centers most on the misinterpretations and shallowness of meaning conveyed in what the press has reported about the Court as a social institution working in such vital modern-day arenas as legislative reapportionment, civil rights for individuals and groups, religion in public schools, public morals and obscenity, or labor-management relations. Thus, throughout this book's critical analysis, stress is given to the problems of interpretation faced by the news media in coverage of such cases as the 1962 New York Regents school prayer decision. Less attention is paid to the obvious and admitted outright errors of fact (perhaps most dramatically represented by the press's momentary confusion in reporting the 1935 Gold Clause cases and the 1956 South Carolina bus desegregation case). Such mistakes and "errors of commission" are obviously important, but they are relatively few in number and fail to reveal many of the significant, long-term Court news coverage problems. It is the "errors of omission" and the "lack of news perspective" that critics of press performance most often attack and worry about.

A FEELING THAT SOMETHING IS WRONG

Apart from the formal and direct criticism of the press on its coverage of the Supreme Court concern is expressed that could best be described as impressionistic and indirect. In total, this criticism provides at least partial support to the occasional statement that the United States Supreme Court is the "least understood of all our governmental institutions." [5] Clearly, evidence indicts more than just the press in this communication problem. The Court itself, the organized bar, the educator, the public official, and the community leader must also share the responsibility for such data as the following:

Only 26 per cent of the population sampled in a 1956 National

5. Among the many who have expressed this view is Chief Justice Earl Warren himself. See especially editorial writer Gilbert Cranberg's two articles based partly on interviews with the Chief Justice: "What Did the Supreme Court Say?" *Saturday Review*, April 8, 1967, 90–92; and "The Court and Its Public: Warren's View," *Des Moines Register*, Oct. 16, 1966. A very general statement by the Chief Justice on the basic problems of Court news coverage can be found in *Report of Committees*, 1966 annual meeting of the AALS, pp. 331–32.

Opinion Research Center poll could give an accurate answer to the question of what the Bill of Rights is. Another 9 per cent admitted they had never even heard of the Bill of Rights;

Only 19 per cent of the sample in a 1952 American Institute of Public Opinion (Gallup) poll could accurately identify the three branches of government;

Only about 40 per cent (in a 1945 Gallup poll) could give the correct number of justices on the United States Supreme Court, compared with only 55 per cent on the same date who could name the number of United States Senators from their state;

Only 14 per cent of the population (in a 1963 Gallup poll) knew about a proposal to create a "Court of the Union"—made up of the 50 state chief justices—that could override decisions of the United States Supreme Court.

Care must be taken, of course, in trying to interpret survey data that cover the full range of society's participants and non-participants. Problems in comparability of findings and changes in knowledge levels over a given period of time, especially, can affect the meaningfulness of these figures. But when such patterns are linked to the belief that publics in a democracy should be informed about main developments in law, the feeling left is an uneasy one, indeed.

> Because the public does not understand the full import and meaning of the judiciary's work, the great and historic decisions that ought to be clarifying the most basic issues in our civil life are, all too often, sources of strife, division and controversy. And this leads not only to uninformed attacks on our judges, but also reduces the vast educational potential of our higher courts to an echo, if not a whimper.[6]

Such concern, as expressed by United States Appellate Court Judge Irving R. Kaufman, is sometimes carried to a more alarming extreme: that public misunderstanding is a real threat to the nation's entire legal system. For example, the practice of judicial candor, Law Professor Paul A. Freund has warned, "presupposes a mature people who in the end will judge their judges rationally. Unless this maturity

6. "The Press, the Courts, and the Law Schools; Toward Justice and an Informed Public," Address, Tulane Law Review Association, New Orleans, April 29, 1965. (Also repeated in speech at seminar for newly appointed U. S. district judges, Denver, July 2, 1965.)

exists, the whole system is in danger of breaking down." [7] And Professor Carl B. Swisher has added: "[The Constitution] can function properly only in a setting of informed public opinion. It cannot function in an intellectual vacuum or, at any rate, in a vacuum as to forceful and stable public sentiment. Government in the absence of such a body of sentiment lacks the positive support which gives it validity and falls prey to the erratic influences which beat upon it. It is like a ship without either rudder or anchor." [8]

THE ANALYTICAL FRAMEWORK

The assumption throughout this book is that the news media serve as only one part of the total communication process. Therefore, in the research design, this analysis stresses what have been called the "strategic points of transmission." [9] By such a definitional standard, the Court's decision-making and opinion-writing processes and final communicated product are all essential in this total communication setting. So, too, are Court efforts at secrecy or attitudes of aloofness, while at the other end of the communication chain are such factors as readers' or listeners' interest, diffusion of information to others, and unintended distortion or deliberate bias. [10]

There is one basic concept that should be stressed briefly here. It is simply that the major purpose of any communication is to convey meaning and that, therefore, the major concern of the news media is (or should be) meaning. In turn, the assumption is that meaning comes through the acquisition and absorption of more than just facts and happenings—or specifically, it also comes through ideas, concepts and perspectives.

The press has significant opportunities to provide meaning. And it must provide meaning. As former Ford Foundation President Henry

7. "The Supreme Court Under Attack," *University of Pittsburgh Law Review,* 25(1963): 7.

8. *The Growth of Constitutional Power in the United States* (Chicago: University of Chicago Press, 1963), p. 188.

9. From especially: Elihu Katz and Paul Lazarsfeld, *Personal Influence* (Glencoe, Ill.: Free Press, 1955).

10. The primary sources, research concepts, and methodology used in this analysis are outlined and summarized in the Bibliographic Note, the Bibliography, and the Appendixes.

T. Heald commented in 1965, when announcing the first of a series of major grants to journalism education:

> The job of assuring a free flow of news and informed comment in a democratic society is infinitely more difficult than it has been.
> Massive social, political and scientific changes, including changes in the techniques of communication itself, make it all the more essential that the people are rapidly and reliably informed.
> American journalism has made great contributions to a free society. To match and surpass this record under conditions of rapid change will require an even greater degree of skill and knowledge among the men who process the news in all its forms.[11]

Or perhaps as significant are the comments of Heald's successor, McGeorge Bundy, in 1967:

> The American press needs to start prizing its readers more and its headlines less. This does not mean less legwork—it means more. It does not mean less contact with government—but more. But it also means visits to universities, better use of libraries, more control of foreign languages, and a refusal to think of all reality only in its relation to the lead.
> We are moving toward the age of the college-trained majority. The American journalist has already entered that age himself. Is it not time for him to deepen his perceptions and raise his sights—to fit his own quality and that of his readers? . . .[12]

To these critical commentaries, finally, perhaps one more judgment should be added—that of Leo Rosten—writer, social scientist, and social critic:

> There is the myth that communication is a fairly common phenomenon which involves a fairly common set of skills. I submit to you that communication is extremely rare; that we really don't know very much about how to get an idea from one head into another. In the effort to communicate we are doing what? We communicate data reasonably well—the multiplication tables, names of rivers, etc. We communicate skills reasonably well—how to build a bookcase or how to tie your shoelaces or how to type. We communicate values fairly well. But we communicate ideas, I think, rather poorly. . . . Because in all our talk about communication we make a fatal assumption: that there is someone trying to communicate something to somebody who wants to listen.[13]

11. Quoted in the *New York Times*, April 21, 1965.
12. Address before the American Society of Newspaper Editors, Washington, D.C., April 20, 1967, published in part, in the *Quill*, June, 1967, p. 66.
13. "The Myths by Which We Live," *Vital Speeches*, April 15, 1965, p. 412.

Herein lies much of the rationale of this book. Not only *can* the challenge of communication be applied to law, but also it *should* be applied. Because, to echo social scientist Harold Lasswell, "One task of a rationally organized society is to discover and control any factors that interfere with effective communication." [14]

14. "The Structure and Function of Communication in Society," in Lyman Bryson (ed.), *The Communication of Ideas* (New York: Harper & Brothers, 1948), p. 46.

II

The Court
as a Communicator

Origins and Limits of the Powers of the Supreme Court

THE SUPREME COURT functions as a moderator deciding a legal issue while at the same time trying to improve the situation that might have created the issue. It seeks to avert the gross miscarriage of justice, to interpret laws, and to make rulings more uniform. It is a "settler of disputes." [1]

But perhaps the most important function of the Supreme Court can be described by the sweeping but troublesome phrase "judicial review" —the checking of some other court's action. This function is unclear partly because it is so discretionary. One striking characteristic of the modern Court is its ability to control, to a large extent, both the volume and substance of the litigation that comes before it. The primary source of this control is the Judiciary Act of 1925; but,

---

1. Interpretations of what the Supreme Court is and does, of course, vary greatly. Among the specific sources used to set up this theme of the Court as a communicator are: Paul A. Freund, "The Supreme Court Crisis," *New York State Bar Bulletin*, 31(1959): 69; Herbert Jacob, *Justice in America* (Boston: Little, Brown and Co., 1965); Jack W. Peltason, *Federal Courts in the Political Process* (Garden City, N. Y.: Doubleday & Co., 1955); John R. Schmidhauser, *The Supreme Court* (New York: Holt, Rinehart, and Winston, 1960); Carl B. Swisher, *The Supreme Court in Modern Role* (New York: New York University Press, 1958 and 1965 editions); and C. Herman Pritchett, *The American Constitution* (New York: McGraw-Hill, 1959).

10

properly, the actual origin of judicial review should be traced back long before the Constitution to its common-law heritage.

It is especially this discretionary ability to grant or deny certiorari (a higher court order to a lower court to bring forth documents of a case) that is the source of so much Supreme Court power. The Court may have to wait for a legal issue to work its way up through the lower courts, but the main issues usually get there eventually. And the Court has the advantage of being able to deny a hearing on an issue which can be considered afresh in some later case.

The Court is obviously an interpreter of the Constitution—a role making it the long-term developer of the law. As Professor Carl B. Swisher wrote: "However careful our reading of constitutions and statutes, we have had the feeling that we know the law only when we had it through official judicial interpretations. It has been, almost, indeed, as if there were no law, but only the potentiality of law, until judges articulated or 'found,' its interpretation." Until the courts act, there are only opinions and guesses as to what the law is.

This task is made even more difficult for the Supreme Court because the Constitution itself is a flexible document subject to wide ranges of interpretation. This flexibility is one reason that the Constitution has endured; but it also is, obviously, a source of possible confusion. One problem of American politics obviously has been the exact meaning of the American Constitution.

The Court has been called a conscience of the people, an enforcer of norms, a potent and omnipresent teacher, a policy-maker, and a political body. But whatever the label, positive and negative, the Supreme Court is one of the most powerful institutions in the United States simply because, to quote Professor Swisher, it

> operates at the storm center of our national life . . . manifests the loftiness of our constitutional ideals . . . touches us to the quick at the focal points of our basic drives as economic, racial, political, and military groups and as a democracy, and . . . displays the diversity of the human menagerie in which all of us play a part.

In such a human menagerie, it is not surprising that the functions and powers of the Supreme Court are a complex mixture of fact and illusion. Clearly, the Court has "veto power" whereby it can challenge Congress or the President and often win. Indeed, it is blessed with the "doctrine of finality"—what the Court says often becomes quickly and simply the "law of the land." But, at the same time, it has an even greater but less obvious impact:

> The momentum of the Court's influence has been achieved imperceptibly, like the gradual growth of a coral reef, as the cumulative product of hundreds of cases, individually unexciting and seemingly even unimportant, but in their total effect powerfully telling in the pulls and pressures of society.[2]

All such influences are very real. Yet, at this point much of the illusion enters, because without the people's respect the Court is virtually powerless. "The Court's authority—possessed of neither the purse nor the sword—ultimately rests on sustained public confidence in its moral sanction." [3] The Court relies heavily on prestige because it has no physical power to enforce its own rulings and no power of taxation; it receives its financial support, including salaries, from Congress. While salaries cannot be reduced, the size of the Court can be—and has been—varied because of legislative action. And, in theory, if not in practice, the Court is subject to some control by the people both through the amending process and through impeachment.

Although the Court has great latitude in determining what cases it will hear, there is an element of illusion here, too. There must be real issues presented before the Court in a real case with real adversaries. Only the litigation before the Court is to be decided; there are no advisory opinions. The Court cannot actively seek out issues; it must wait for them to work their ways through the judicial process.

Furthermore, perhaps as importantly, there is the restriction that while the Supreme Court may provide the final judicial decision it does not necessarily provide the final judicial action. Adversely affected interests before the Court can regain victory in lower courts. The Supreme Court normally returns a case to trial judges by way of intermediate appellate courts. It is often these trial judges who have to interpret and apply the Supreme Court's ruling. For example, between 1941 and 1951, out of 175 cases which the Supreme Court reversed and remanded to state tribunals, there were 46 cases involving further litigation. Of these 46, about half turned out to be reversed.

2. Felix Frankfurter, *Mr. Justice Holmes and the Supreme Court* (Cambridge, Mass.: Harvard University Press, 1938), p. 3.
3. Justice Frankfurter in *Baker* v. *Carr*, 369 U.S. 186, 267 (1962).

In other words, "Even for the immediate parties, a Supreme Court victory is not cause for too much celebration." As between the interests, a Supreme Court victory for one "hardly means that the other lost the war." [4]

Many other examples of such limits on Supreme Court power can be found. A common one is the convicted criminal (such as in *Miranda* v. *Arizona*) who may have won a temporary victory in the Supreme Court but who is reconvicted in a retrial. Or there are the civil rights cases that may go back to Southern courts and get bogged down in a slow process of rehearings. Sometimes there is deliberate feet-dragging here or looking the other way; but, more times than not, the assignment from the Supreme Court may be too "awesome" —such as the difficult task for Southern judges in forcing compliance with the Supreme Court's 1954 school desegregation decision.[5]

PSYCHOLOGICAL SOURCES OF POWER

More difficult to trace are concepts of power that are even more illusive and elusive—what people may *think* the Court is or does. Here is image often based on impressions or, as Walter Lippmann observed years ago in his *Public Opinion*, on stereotypes and "the pictures in our heads."

Part of the Court's power, for example, comes from the great public respect or even reverence for the law. Included here is what might be called the myth of a government of laws, not men. This concept, although largely true as a statement of the American heritage, has never been very satisfactory as a realistic and literal description of the political process; indeed, it would seem better to say that laws are "made, enforced, and interpreted by men." [6]

The Supreme Court and the justices usually operate in an atmosphere of prestige and public awe. In both the 1947 and the 1963 National

4. Figures and conclusion from Peltason, *Federal Courts in the Political Process,* p. 60.

5. From Gordon Patric, "The Impact of a Court Decision: Aftermath of the McCollum Case," *Journal of Public Law,* 6(1957): 464; and J. W. Peltason, *Fifty-Eight Lonely Men* (New York: Harcourt, Brace & World, 1961), pp. 3–29.

6. Robert G. McCloskey, *The American Supreme Court* (Chicago: University of Chicago Press, 1960), *passim;* and Schmidhauser, *The Supreme Court,* p. 6.

Opinion Research Center surveys of opinion about occupational prestige, the occupation of Supreme Court justice ranked first. Except for the Presidency (not included on either survey list), it probably can be said that the job of Supreme Court justice is as prestigious as any that a man can hold.

One result of this situation is a widespread expectation as to judicial behavior. "When a man becomes a judge he is expected to stand somewhat above the contests in the community, and if he is appointed to the Supreme Court he is elevated so high that for most of the populace he is 'at least brushed with divinity.' " [7]

Out of all this come sometimes significant myths about the Court that can interfere with public understanding of the judicial process. For example:

> The myth of depersonalized and machinelike adjudication upon which rests in part the continued popular acceptance of the judicial function assumes that all . . . attachments are left behind when a man ascends the bench. . . . This assumption has some limited basis in fact. It is strengthened by the effect of membership in the judicial group. This effect is in the nature of modification, however, not of a transformation. Judges do not cease to be human when they don their robes. [8]

The judicial robe itself is a symbol that provides an image of prestige, protection, and uniformity; it gives a feeling of formal authority and control. Nine black-robed justices create an image of equal justice under law. Probably except for the Constitution itself, the Supreme Court is the country's greatest symbol of orderly and stable government. [9]

The important point is that throughout this symbolism is an element of mystique. The law has become a potent if often ambiguous symbol, withdrawn from everyday life except as seen on occasion in the form of courts, police, and prisons. The result is that the very nature of law "gets in the way of realistic observation of the workings and significance of law." [10]

7. David B. Truman, *The Governmental Process* (New York: Alfred A. Knopf, 1951), p. 483.

8. *Ibid.*, p. 490.

9. Alpheus T. Mason, "Myth and Reality in Supreme Court Decisions," *Virginia Law Review*, 48(1962): 1387.

10. Richard Snyder, Editor's Foreword in Victor G. Rosenblum, *Law as a Political Instrument* (New York: Random House, 1955), p. iii.; Jerome Frank, *Law and the Modern Mind* (New York: Brentano's, 1930), p. 91.

Much of this mystique about the Court can interfere with real public understanding. The point here is not to argue for or against Court symbolism, ritual, and tradition but simply to note that such psychological forces can be among the "intervening variables" in complicating the communication chain from the written opinion of a justice through the mass news media to the reader, viewer, or listener. In turn, the information and understanding finally absorbed from the media and through personal influences are significant in determining an individual's judgment of the wisdom of a Court decision. The process then turns full cycle since such collective judgments of public opinion partly influence the Court and the long-term effectiveness of law.

SECRECY AND ALOOFNESS

Closely related to the principle of mystical power is the deliberate isolation of the Court from the public. There is little doubt that much of this isolation is needed to protect the judicial process; but the point, again, is that such practices also help to complicate communication between institution and citizen.

The justices and Court staff go to great lengths to keep decisions secret until announced in the courtroom. The reasons involve both tradition and necessity; Court decisions often involve important issues and the slightest leak could affect the stock market or the proper procedures for the administration of justice. Opinions obviously are also guarded because the Court was meant to be independent. No outside forces, it is argued, should be allowed to interfere with judicial decision-making. Groups or individuals should not act before the Court has officially stated its position. The Court should be as free as possible from all external pressures.

More than just the sacredness of the law is involved here, however. For example, it seems logical that parties in the suit should be the first to know how their case has been resolved. The first objective of the Court is to decide the case before it. To release information in advance of the official announcement would be to ignore this primary responsibility to the parties involved.

Equally important is the philosophy behind the legal opinion—

that it should "stand alone." Only the words written and nothing else should be handed down as "the law" in a case. Also, until the decision is announced in the courtroom, a member of the Court is free to change his mind. Maximum time in considering a case is sought, including the last-minute chance for a change of heart.

Court procedures to protect secrecy—such as the private deliberation by the justices in the conference room—have often been sketched. In sum, the evolving and final written opinions of the Court are available to no one except the justices themselves and a few Court staff until that moment in the courtroom when a justice begins, "I have for announcement the decision of the Court in. . . ."

Even critics of the Court seem to agree strongly with this protection of the Court's business. But one cannot deny that such secretiveness does not further public dialogue and understanding about Court decisions and how they were reached.

Nor is there much potential for understanding with the physical and social barriers built up around justices. Except for the President, there is probably no group of public leaders more isolated in Washington. "Great bronze doors literally exclude the public from the reaches of the marble building where most of the work is done." [11] Seven of the justices' offices are sealed off behind these doors and protected by guards. Two suites are just outside these doors along a semi-public corridor and are also carefully protected. In either setting, visitors with appointments must go to the marshal's office before they can be permitted to see a member of the Court. This policy obviously makes sense but is in marked contrast to the nearby Senate and House office buildings, which allow considerable freedom of public movement. Also, the Supreme Court is much more isolated than other judicial levels; for example, most judges in United States Courts of Appeals have chambers adjoining their receptionist's office.

The whole physical appearance of the Supreme Court Building and of the courtroom, in fact, make the visitor feel overpowered and awestruck. Despite very human goings-on within the building, the long marble corridors, high ceilings, solid pillars, and symbolic statues and

11. Anthony Lewis, "The Justices' Supreme Job," *New York Times Magazine*, June 11, 1961. Other details in this section come from personal interviews, observation, and, in part, from Paul F. Healy, "Backstage at the Supreme Court," *Saturday Evening Post*, Jan. 2, 1960, pp. 22–23; 49–55.

friezes all convey an image of grandiose detachment from the commonplace world.

Such impressions, too, are reinforced when the visitor has the chance to watch the justices in action in the courtroom. The traditions and rituals of the Court are steeped in history; for example, the chant of the Court Marshal as the justices step forward into the courtroom at 10 A.M. sharp on a hearing or opinion-announcing day:

> The Honorable, the Chief Justice and Associate Justices of the Supreme Court of the United States! Oyez, Oyez, Oyez! All persons having business before the Honorable, the Supreme Court of the United States are admonished to draw near and give their attention, for the Court is now sitting. God save the United States and this Honorable Court.

Except in the courtroom, the justices are seldom seen in public areas of the Supreme Court Building. They have a private dining room and usually enter and leave through rear or side exits to the staff parking lot. Supreme Court justices are for the most part simply kept out of public sight.

APPROACHES TOWARD PUBLIC RELATIONS

Justices are not totally inaccessible and silent, of course. In fact, during recent years members of the Court have become more accessible, giving more speeches and making more public appearances.[12] Reasons behind this wearing off of protectiveness can be traced to various specific factors, such as the 1937 Court-packing battle which broke down some of the myths that had previously secluded the courts. More recently the news media have generally opened up areas of government news as seldom before. Presidents, senators, and justices alike have

12. Conclusion based mostly on a rough secondary analysis of "A Selected Bibliography of Speeches and Extrajudicial Writings by United States Supreme Court Justices," in Alan F. Westin (ed.), *An Autobiography of the Supreme Court* (New York: Macmillan Co., 1963), pp. 35–47. Projections based on similar public commentary for the post–1962 periods indicate that the justices have maintained this high level. Of the ten all-time most active members of the Court in speaking and writing through 1962, four are current or very recent: Douglas ranked first, Frankfurter third, Warren sixth, and Clark tenth. Chief Justice Hughes ranked second and Justices Robert H. Jackson and Samuel P. Miller were tied for fourth.

all been placed in positions of having to say they welcome criticism and public scrutiny.

Even more important in the decline of judicial immunity, however, have been the activist trends of the Court reflected among recent members. Chief Justice Earl Warren, for example, has been very much the politician aware of the importance of public appearances, while Justice Tom Clark was reputed to be a "practitioner's judge," making himself available as a "counselor" and supporter of bar associations and law-enforcement groups. There have been the voluminous speech-makings and writings and out-going styles of a Felix Frankfurter, an Arthur Goldberg, and a William O. Douglas. And there has been the behind-the-scenes activism of an Abe Fortas, still very much the counselor and occasional "aide" of President Lyndon Johnson.[13]

In recent years, too, there have been more occasional breaks from the custom of no out-of-Court commentary. Most notable was Justice Clark's public defense of the 1962 New York Regents school prayer decision.[14] Even Justice Hugo Black at that time departed from his normal practice of not replying to critics and answered some letters that came to him.[15]

But despite all such changes in approach to public appearances and commentary, there still are many self-imposed restrictions on what is said out of the courtroom. Whether the group being addressed is a touring high school class or a bar association convention, justices usually limit their remarks to procedural and general constitutional matters. Controversy is usually avoided. (One of the best examples is Chief Justice Warren's preoccupation with the topic of international law, which allows him to avoid awkward matters about the Court and to stress instead such "safe" themes as world peace.)

Such restrictions can be a frustrating experience for a member of the Court. One reason a justice doesn't speak more often in public is

13. See especially, Fred P. Graham, "The Many-Sided Justice Fortas," *New York Times Magazine*, June 4, 1967, pp. 26–27, 86–89.

14. Address before the Commonwealth Club of San Francisco, Aug. 3, 1962, reported in some detail in the *Washington Post*, Aug. 4, 1962. Justice Clark also repeated much of this criticism in a speech on Sept. 23, 1962, before the Churchman's Association, Larchmont Avenue Church, Larchmont, N. Y.

15. James E. Clayton, *The Making of Justice* (New York: E. P. Dutton & Co., 1964), p. 21.

that there is a limit to what he can say. The justices are aware that often there is nothing they can say. Sometimes in such a situation the most satisfactory solution is to reject most public-speaking invitations.

Perhaps the most frustrating part is the criticism because the judge is traditionally not supposed to speak up to defend himself.[16] Thus it is not surprising that on occasion justices do speak out—if not directly, then indirectly. Sometimes the public statements will take the defensive approach of "clarifying a misconception," such as pointing out that the Court does not pass on cases by a committee system or that it cannot reach out for issues but must instead wait for them to come before it.[17] Or the justice may be involved in mild advocacy. For example, Chief Justice Warren has frequently cited the words written across the front of the Supreme Court Building, "Equal Justice Under Law," in his public speeches and writings. The clear impression is that the Chief Justice believes this motto means exactly what it says and should be stressed.

But even in vaguely supporting their causes, members of the Court must be careful to stay within the bounds of propriety. The result is that sometimes the public statements of a justice on a subject may not match his private feelings at all. Sometimes erratic patterns of public exposure are the results, and, again, barriers to understanding between the Court and the many publics interested in it are built. In overview: "All of official Washington except the Supreme Court is acutely conscious of public relations. The Supreme Court is about as oblivious as it is conceivable to be." [18] A good case can be made that such lack of public relations and promotion is a desirable philosophy for the protection of the legal institution. And yet, as Chief Jus-

16. Robert A. Leflar, "The Task of the Appellate Court," *Notre Dame Lawyer,* 33(1958): 572.

17. Some public misconceptions about Court procedures are apparently long-lasting. In 1896, for example, Justice John Marshall Harlan tried to advise the bar that there was no committee system in deciding cases (Address, reported in *American Law Review,* 30[1896]: 903–4). About sixty years later it was ironic that his grandson, the current Justice John Marshall Harlan, felt it necessary to make roughly the same clarification in a public speech (Westin, *Autobiography of the Supreme Court,* pp. 8–9).

18. Anthony Lewis, "Problems of a Washington Correspondent," *Connecticut Bar Journal,* 33(1959): 365.

tice Charles E. Hughes observed in 1938, something of a dilemma is created:

> The courts have no advertiser, they have no one to publicize the extent of their industry; they work quietly, their work cannot be understood by many, and the reasons for decisions in many cases are beyond public comprehension. It is of vital importance that every step should be taken to keep the work of the courts so far as possible in the good opinion of the country. It is of greatest importance that everything should be done to conserve the confidence of the people in the administration of justice. . . .[19]

Ironically, thus, the Court needs good relations with the public but is in a position where it cannot do much directly to improve these relations—or at least it feels it cannot do much. As a result of such a philosophy sometimes there are no relations at all or there is a tendency to try to avoid the whole problem by doing nothing about it; in the extreme the Court may even try to pretend the publics are not there at all. In contrast to Congressmen, who may think in terms of headlines,[20] the justices seem to ignore much of what will be written about their opinions.

In some situations there is considerable public attention prior to a decision. The 1954 school desegregation case is such an example. The case was heard and reheard by the Court, and, when the decision was finally handed down, the Court withheld releasing the written opinion until the whole text could be read aloud in the courtroom by Chief Justice Warren. Such an easing-in process and "news sense" seem to be the exception, however. Instead of gradual focus on issues, most Court opinions come as "bolts from a hazy blue." [21] For example, many critics and observers of the Court cite the shock of the 1962 school prayer decision as an important factor in the uproar and confusion that followed the release of that decision to the public.

The Court is not blind to such possible shock effects of its decisions, but the evidence is that it would indeed prefer to ignore the conse-

19. The Judicial Proceedings of the Judicial Conference, Sept. 30, 1938, on the Administrative Office Bill, pp. 174–92 (Extract, p. 13).

20. Suggested especially by Bernard C. Cohen, *The Press and Foreign Policy* (Princeton, N.J.: Princeton University Press, 1963), p. 205.

21. As phrased by Anthony Lewis, "How the Supreme Court Reaches Decisions," *New York Times Magazine*, Dec. 1, 1957, p. 51.

quences. Interviews around the Court Building—with two justices (who were willing to have their remarks attributed to members of the Court), the Court's Press Officer, the Clerk of the Court, and the Administrator of the Federal Courts—indicate clearly that there is a deliberate effort to avoid appearing to be in the business of widespread dissemination of judicial opinions. The wisdom of such a "hands off" policy can be argued pro and con, but the important point is that there is little active effort to disseminate Court opinions and apparently little machinery set up to anticipate possibly controversial cases. There are few clear lines of authority for public relations activities; both the Press Officer and Clerk of the Court have some public relations-type obligations, but neither sees his job as at all promotional in nature.

Copies of opinions are not routinely sent out in any large numbers. Individuals may request copies through the Press Officer or Clerk's Office, or through the United States Government Printing Office, but the general policy of the Court staff is that it should not take the initiative in disseminating information about the Court. The one major exception to this policy is the effort made to contact parties involved in cases before the Court. The Clerk's Office notifies the litigants immediately of the outcome and sends along a copy of the decision. In addition, during recent years the large number of due-process cases has brought many requests from prisoners for copies of opinions. Court staff say they have made special efforts to send out a "reasonable number" of opinions to persons isolated in prisons who might be directly affected by a recent Court decision. The number of such requests varies greatly, but the figure sometimes runs as high as 150 to 200 per week.

Whether the Court should be more involved in informational publicity is a complex question beyond the scope of this book. But the "whys" of current practice can be appropriately isolated here. In sum, the administration of justice demands objectivity and independence. The Court, it is argued, should be above the commonplace of image-making or of forcing its opinions on others.

But there is another factor that should be considered, a different view that sees power as partly the ability to control the flow of information about government. In general, the stream of communication is an instrument by which the powerful protect their power and position.[22]

By not *trying* to manipulate public opinion, the Court paradoxically *is* manipulating public opinion. The Court controls the flow of news by releasing only what it wants to say and by often leaving vague what it does not want to say. There is no direct answer from the public. No press conference nor defenses are needed. The Court simply speaks and the country and parts of the world listen. Thus, while it can be argued that the Court shows great self-restraint and wisdom by being silent, it also can be observed that this silence may serve best the Court's self-interest. Not only may the Court feel it does not need or should not have public relations, it may also simply not want public relations.

How a Case Is Decided and an Opinion Written

A Difficult Task

It has been observed that the job of understanding the Supreme Court "forces lawyers to become philosophers." [23] Much of what lawyers and judges do may be fairly routine and easy to understand. But in many situations and especially at the Supreme Court the decisions are "delicate and imponderable, complex and tangled. They require at times the economist's understanding, the poet's insight, the executive's experience, the political scientist's understanding, the historian's perspective." [24]

> When the Court itself is in a quandary about its own performance, it is not surprising that laymen should be deeply bewildered and should jump to the over-simplified conclusion that the Court is utterly erratic or is following nothing but individual biases or is yielding to the pres-

22. Francis E. Rourke, *Secrecy and Publicity* (Baltimore: Johns Hopkins Press, 1961), p. vii; and Harold D. Lasswell, "Describing the Effects of Communication," in Bruce Lannes Smith, Harold D. Lasswell, and Ralph D. Casey, *Propaganda, Communication, and Public Opinion* (Princeton, N. J.: Princeton University Press, 1946), p. 113.

23. Paul A. Freund, *On Understanding the Supreme Court* (Boston: Little Brown and Co., 1949), p. 7.

24. William O. Douglas, "The Supreme Court and Its Case Load," *Cornell Law Quarterly*, 45(1960): 414.

sures of the hour. . . . Yet close observation indicates that it is a quandary produced by almost insoluble problems rather than by mere political-mindedness. . . .[25]

Of course, many critics feel the Court's task has become especially complex for reasons other than just the issues faced. For example, in the complex area of religion in the schools, it is sometimes argued that the public has the "right to be appalled" by some of the Court's inconsistent decisions over time.

The important point is that the Court's ability to change its mind is important in the democratic process but that this is a flexibility with the possible price of public confusion and misunderstanding. In turn, such confusion and misunderstanding brings on much of the heated criticism and unsophisticated praise of the Court.

Without attempting to judge the Court in this controversy about its consistency, it is proper to note that it faces the difficult assignment of wrestling with the meaning and application of the law. As Justice Frankfurter noted in *Baker* v. *Carr* in 1962, so many questions of law are "matters of degree." The need to draw fine lines and to provide shades of interpretation in legal issues simply is bound to leave both close and distant observers of the Court with doubts and frustrations.

Perhaps no area better illustrates the problem than the task of interpreting the meaning of the Constitution and statutes. "The Constitution is expressed in language which ranges from statements so precise as to be nearly indisputable, through ambiguity and vague generality, to failure to say anything where one might think a statement is clearly needed." [26]

The acts of Congress or legislatures may be no better: the language of statutes is often unclear. Even when the draftsmanship is excellent, the statute may be worded in generalities which furnish no definite guide when courts must apply it to the circumstances of particular cases.[27] (Here is, indeed, an ironic circular problem in which the courts may be caught. Legislatures may end up deliberately draft-

25. Swisher, *The Supreme Court in Modern Role*, p. 185.
26. Charles Hyneman, *The Supreme Court on Trial* (New York: Atherton Press, 1963), pp. 67–68.
27. C. Herman Pritchett, *Congress Versus the Supreme Court* (Minneapolis: University of Minnesota Press, 1961), p. 128.

ing ambiguous statutes as a means of shifting pressure to the courts. Then, when the courts step in to try to interpret the ambiguity, the legislatures may cry that their power is being usurped or that their intent has been misunderstood.)

Words change in meaning over time, too. Thus, the instability of the legal document becomes a fundamental part of the justices' decision-making problems. "Nothing is stable. Nothing absolute. All is fluid and changeable. There is an endless becoming.' " [28]

Legal Reasoning: The Decision-Making Process

The work of deciding cases goes on every day in hundreds of courts throughout the land. Any judge, one might suppose, would find it easy to describe the process which he had followed a thousand times and more. Nothing could be farther from the truth. Let some intelligent layman ask him to explain: he will not go very far before taking refuge in the excuse that the language of craftsmen is unintelligible to those untutored in the craft. Such an excuse may cover with a semblance of respectability an otherwise ignominious retreat. It will hardly serve to still the pricks of curiosity and conscience. [29]

Some broad outlines of legal decision-making, fortunately, can be made. For example, the basic analytical pattern is reasoning by example—reasoning from case to case. [30] Here, the process of precedent involves documenting the first case, making it the rule of law, and then applying it to the second case. The main ingredients in this method are rationality and logic.

Obviously, the total process is not quite so simple. Judge Jerome Frank explained the problem with a psychological slant that some may dispute but which nevertheless goes a long way in providing needed insight:

The process of judging, so the psychologists tell us, seldom begins with a premise from which a conclusion is subsequently worked out. Judging begins rather the other way around—with a conclusion more or less vaguely formed; a man ordinarily starts with such a conclusion and

28. Benjamin N. Cardozo, *The Nature of the Judicial Process* (New Haven: Yale University Press, 1921), p. 28.
29. *Ibid.*, p. 9.
30. Main reference used for this section is Edward H. Levi, *An Introduction to Legal Reasoning* (Chicago: University of Chicago Press, 1948).

afterwards tries to find premises which will substantiate it. If he cannot, to his satisfaction, find proper arguments to link up his conclusion with premises, which he finds acceptable, he will, unless he is arbitrary or mad, reject the conclusion and seek another.

While "the dominance of the conclusion" in the case of the lawyer is clear, it is less so in the case of the judge. For the respectable and traditional description of the judicial judging process admits no such backward-working explanation. In theory, the judge begins with some rule or principle of the law as his premise, applies the premise to the facts, and thus arrives at his decision. . . .

But . . . judicial judgments, like other judgments, doubtless, in most cases, are worked out backward from conclusions tentatively formulated.[31]

One result of this system is that formal logic can be used in just about any way needed by the judge. For instance, the problem of showing similarity between Case 1 and Case 2 can be all-important. But the approach of logic—using form instead of content—can mask over this difficulty by simply stating that Case 1 applies to Case 2. Formal logic makes the link but it often does not show how strong the connection really is. The result is that the court can decide one way or the other and in either case can make its reasoning appear equally flawless. Or to phrase the result differently: "We have built up such a mass of precedents that by selective use of them we can prove almost anything—which in the end means practically nothing." [32]

This inability to "prove" the law means that the law is never really fully settled. This situation may or may not be desirable, but it certainly is another potential area for confusion among judges, lawyers, public officials, and private citizens.

The whole process also can be complicated when such factors as the individual justice' personality, ideology, and background are added. As Judge Frank argues, efforts to eliminate the personality of the judge are doomed to failure. The best course seems to be to recognize the necessary personal element and to act accordingly.

By comparison, procedural elements in the judicial decision-making process at the Court seem relatively simple. The Court convenes for a new term the first Monday in October—as required by statute—and usually winds up its business for the term in mid-June—as prac-

31. Frank, *Law and the Modern Mind*, p. 101.
32. Swisher, *The Supreme Court in Modern Role*, p. 185.

ticed by tradition. It operates in what might best be described as segments. Once under way in the fall, it will usually hear cases four days a week for two weeks and then recess for about two weeks for decision-writing and other research. Usually during the middle of the term, the Court will recess for a month; then follows the final push in the spring in an effort to get through by the second or third week in June.

The Court operates with clock-conscious efficiency. Public and private group sessions are scheduled for 10 A.M. and are usually no more than a minute or so late. The Court breaks from its public court-room sessions exactly at noon and returns exactly at 12:30. Its finishing time of 2:30 is closely observed.[33]

Before the justices ever get into the courtroom, however, important judicial decisions and selections have been made. One of the most important judicial roles is that of the Solicitor General, who is in charge of deciding which lower court decisions the federal government will appeal to the Supreme Court.

The final crucial selection process at the Court comes when the justices decide to hear or not to hear a case. In matters of certiorari, only four of the nine members of the Court need to vote to hear the case in order to get it on the Court calendar. This selection process gets much less public attention than actual decisions, but it is important and especially time-consuming as the number of petitions filed each year increases. The petitions for certiorari pile up during the summer months. It is then that law clerks for the justices are useful in going through the often lengthy legal briefs and in making preliminary sortings or writing memoranda of highlights for use by the justices. (At the Supreme Court level, of course, as with other appellate levels, no new evidence may be presented. Hearings on any case are based on the record made in the original proceedings.)

During the October–June term, the Court will focus its attention by writing opinions in more than 100 cases. It is these cases, along with more than 50 others which are decided without written opinions,

33. But courtroom observers note that Chief Justice Warren has provided an element of flexibility. He usually will let the lawyer in oral argument finish his sentence or thought after the 60-minute time-limit light has started flashing. This leniency is in marked contrast with the popular tale that some chief justices in the past have been noted to cut off an advocate in the middle of the word "if" or "is."

that make up the Court calendar. This is the time when legal briefs have their minutes of public exposure through oral argument in the courtroom. These 150–175 cases are the "chosen few" (roughly only 5 or 6 per cent of the more than 3,000 cases that the Court must now act on each year).

But, as with legislative and executive branches of government, the real decision-making action does not occur in the public arena. It is away from the courtroom that this takes place—specifically in the 10 A.M. Friday conferences when the justices meet in absolute privacy to discuss the cases heard and the cases that may be argued eventually in the courtroom. At this time, tentative sides are drawn up and the process of selecting opinion writers, drafting opinions, persuasion, and compromise is set in motion.

Proceedings in the oak-paneled, book-lined conference room are entirely secret with no one but the nine justices present. The newest member of the Court acts as the keeper of the door—receiving and sending out messages and notes.[34] What goes on specifically in the conference room is not disclosed; but, in general, the cases are presented one by one by the Chief Justice. He starts the discussion and is the last to vote.[35] A case may be disposed of in a few moments or discussion may be extended for hours. The meetings, usually with a half-hour break for lunch, often last late into the afternoon and sometimes are reconvened on Saturday mornings. After the vote has been taken, it is up to the Chief Justice to assign the case to a member of the Court whose side he is on. If there is a majority or minority not voting with the Chief Justice, the senior justice of that group assigns the opinion. Justices usually are notified of their assignments on the following Monday.

After the Friday session and after the opinions have been assigned,

34. One such message—inning-by-inning World Series scores delivered by messenger to the conference room door. ("The Warren Court: Fateful Decade," *Newsweek*, May 11, 1964, p. 25.)

35. Supposedly, the freshman justice, by voting first, will feel no pressure or will not be influenced by the votes of his seniors. But the philosophy does not always work in practice. As noted by Justice Charles Whittaker: "Everyone knows how the votes are going because we have discussed the case. I remember several occasions when it was obvious that the other eight were going to split even on the opinion, so the monkey was on my back." Quoted in "Highest Court Also Steeped in Tradition," *Chicago Tribune*, Feb. 26, 1967.

there is a constant interchange of communications. Memos are circulated, offices visited, and phones rung. Discussions often are extended to the lunch table. All this goes on until the justices are able to hammer out the final form of each opinion. The end product may come after one writing or may be the labor of as many as ten printed drafts—or even more.[36]

Words and the Law: The Written Product

The writing of an opinion seeks to ensure a thoughtful review of the issues. The immediate function is to explain to the parties involved what is being done with the case; the long-range accomplishment is to help develop and shape the evolution of the law and public policy.

> Opinions are the public voice of appellate courts, and so represent the judiciary to the public, but they are not voices merely. They are what the courts do, not just what they say. They are the substance of judicial action, not just news releases about what the courts have done. . . .[37]

The written opinion itself is somewhat like a legislative debate with obvious pro and con votes, but often it is organized in a more orderly and systematic fashion. As a means of debate, the written opinion helps facilitate acceptance of the decision. It is also a means of reinforcing the power of the Court.

Judges, like legislators, are expected to explain their conduct and to justify their decisions. It is partly this reason that makes an opinion useful.

> Technically, the Court's decision in a case applies only to the particular facts of that case and to the parties to it. But the reasoning outlined by the Court gives lower court judges a basis for deciding similar cases. The Court's effectiveness in guiding the development of American law depends on the quality and clarity of its reasoning and the willingness of lower courts to accept it.[38]

36. Description and details here especially from Justice William J. Brennan, Jr., Address, Maxwell Air Force Base, Alabama, Sept. 1, 1963; reprinted, in general, as: "Inside View of the High Court," *New York Times Magazine*, Oct. 6, 1963, pp. 35, 100–103.

37. Robert A. Leflar, "Some Observations Concerning Judicial Opinions," *Columbia Law Review*, 61(1961): 819.

38. Clayton, *The Making of Justice*, p. 85.

A collective majority or collective dissenting opinions are ways to pool the best possible judicial reasoning while also saving time and energy. In comparison to a system where each justice writes a separate opinion, the method should provide more clarity and decisiveness. It should help to provide maximum weight behind a decision.

The majority opinion gives a chance for ideas to be tested and tempered by the criticism of associates. Instead of extremes, there tends to be moderation—compromise coming from the adding and subtracting process of judicial argumentation.

But even if such moderation is assumed to be a virtue, the system includes built-in difficulties. The writing of an opinion is often a struggle. In the adding and subtracting process, as one legal expert put it, "the choicest morsels are sometimes lost."

At this point an important question arises: For whom are the justices writing opinions? Who are their audiences—or who do they think are their audiences?

A common notion is that judges usually write for posterity and other lawyers. One survey of state and federal appellate judges indicates that there is at least some basis for this belief. The question—"To whom (or for whom) do you write your opinions?"—brought replies in the following order: first, for posterity; second, for the bar; and third, for future judges.[39]

Results of extensive interviewing at the Court Building and nearby, however, indicate that this view may need some modification—at least at the Supreme Court level. The needs for compromise and persuasion in opinion-writing show the importance (for the opinion writer) of other Court members. It can be argued that the Court "is" the bar and to write for one is to write for the other. This view, however, does not account for the complex interaction necessary among the justices before an opinion can take final form.

There is some feeling that the primary audience for the justice writing the majority opinion is the group of justices who might go along with his decision. The justice writing a majority opinion (and some minority and concurring opinions) is writing first to "please" other justices. The decision itself is the most important task of the opinion

39. Cited by Leflar, "Some Observations Concerning Judicial Opinions," pp. 813–14.

writer. Later, or perhaps concurrently, he may consciously or sub-consciously ask himself, "I wonder what the legal profession will think?"

This interpretation cannot be considered necessarily representative of the whole Court.[40] But the two justices who said their comments could be attributed to a member of the Court provide strong support for the view.

On this question of audience, Justice Tom C. Clark said he wrote "largely" for the Court and lawyers—in that order. He was careful to distinguish between the two. He also said he attempted to get as large a majority as possible and would change his wording on occasion to seek that objective.[41] The other justice interviewed ("on the record" but without identification by name) answered the same question by noting that, "after the Court," he writes to satisfy himself and then the litigants, lawyers, and perhaps the few laymen who might be interested.[42] (When a judge is writing to please himself, he is also, of course, writing to please a member of the legal profession.)

Further evidence of this primary group involvement can be found in contrasting multiple opinions of several justices with one-man efforts. This is especially true in a dissent. There are often distinct differences in style between group and individual opinions. The latter simply exhibit more freedom of expression.

As Chief Justice Hughes observed in 1928:

> Dissenting opinions enable a judge to express his individuality. He is not under the compulsion of speaking for the court and thus of securing the concurrence of a majority. In dissenting, he is a free lance. A dissent in a court of last resort is an appeal to the brooding spirit of the law, to the intelligence of a future day. . . .[43]

Dissents tend to be easier to write because there is less responsibility involved. They also "have a way of better pleasing those who read

40. Six of the eight justices interviewed talked on a background-only basis without wanting their comments to be identified as coming from a member of the Court. Thus, summary conclusions about what most of the justices think cannot be made. For details, see the author's "Interviewing at the Court," *Public Opinion Quarterly*, 31(Summer, 1967): 285–89.

41. June 10, 1965, personal interview.

42. May 6, 1965, personal interview.

43. *The Supreme Court of the United States* (New York: Columbia University Press, 1928), p. 68.

as well as those who write them. . . . Opinions which must meet the ideas of many minds may in comparison seem dull and undistinguished." [44]

The dissent, of course, serves as more than just a creative outlet or a chance for judicial self-expression. It may seek to change votes on a pending case and, in fact, on occasion it can do just that—turning a minority view into a majority view. Even if it fails to change opinions, it can serve as a negative voice to restrict the majority opinion. And, of course, whether the author intends it or not, a dissent can become a direct appeal to members of Congress, to the President and lower court judges, to the bar or other interest groups, or to the public at large to change the decision of the majority.[45] Many a minority, over time and after changes in Court personnel, has become the majority.

The concept of dissent has obvious disadvantages. The analytical point here is not the merit or demerit of dissents but the potential effect they may have on the communication of Court decisions. As Justice Robert Jackson pointed out:

> There has been much undiscriminating eulogy of dissenting opinions. It is said they clarify issues. Often they do the exact opposite. The technique of the dissenter often is to exaggerate the holding of the Court beyond the meaning of the majority and then to blast away at the excess.[46]

The writing of a dissent or of a concurring opinion can affect greatly the understanding of what the Court has said in the majority opinion. The internal clash among the majority, concurring, and minority opinions sometimes helps to focus on the main issues; but just as likely, it causes confusion. This resulting uncertainty or clouding of issues is part of the more basic problem of "legal language," which in turn is obviously a major element in the total problem of communicating Supreme Court decisions.

44. Robert H. Jackson, "The Law Is a Rule for Men to Live By," *Vital Speeches,* June 23, 1943, p. 665.

45. Walter Murphy, *Elements of Judicial Strategy* (Chicago: University of Chicago Press, 1960), p. 60.

46. Robert H. Jackson, *The Supreme Court in the American System of Government* (New York: Harper Torchbooks, 1963), pp. 18–19.

Justice Whittaker is among those who have forcefully focused on this problem of words for the lawyer and judge:

> I believe we ought to be able to agree that words—though not ends in themselves—are our only tool and means of communicating thoughts and ideas. Hence plain and unambiguous words surely should be taken and adhered to in their commonly accepted sense, for otherwise the result must necessarily be the loss of all means of communicating with certainty; and all documents, however carefully prepared, would become mere "scraps of paper." [47]

Every appellate judge is, in a sense, a "professional writer." Clearly, the way a justice writes is vital in the interest of administration of the law. And clearly, a justice' stature and place in history depend partly on the clarity of his analysis and the power of his words. Here is a view of the Supreme Court justice as, partly, a "worker with words." [48]

Legal writing, as a crucial part of the legal decision process, is committed to the philosophy of thoroughness in research and detailed building-up and tearing-down—and sometimes ignoring—of precedent. In this demanding setting, it is perhaps inevitable there should be at least some "gobbledygook" in legal prose. It is a style that often incorporates a "double language"—using essentially the same words at times to say and decide issues two different ways. [49]

In defense, such a style of involved and obscure writing is not unique, of course, to lawyers and judges (academic writers are perhaps the masters of such complex verbal devices). It also would be easy to defend the justices on the basis that today's legal system is so complex and ingrained that any other form of communication would be too much to expect. After all, judges are supposed to be temperate in language and to avoid any bias; they are supposed to phrase their decisions and explain them in language which conceals any subjective elements.

47. "A Confusion of Tongues," *American Bar Association Journal*, 51(January, 1965): 28.
48. This section is based on personal interviews; cf. also Anthony Lewis, "What Quality for the Court?" *New York Times Magazine*, Oct. 6, 1957, p. 101; and Glenn Leggett, "Judicial Writing: An Observation by a Teacher of Writing," *Law Library Journal*, 58(May, 1965): 115.
49. Stuart Chase, *Power of Words* (New York: Harcourt, Brace and Co., 1954), p. 251; and Frank, *Law and the Modern Mind*, p. 28.

But despite such defenses, critics can quickly point out the resulting problems:

> The average judicial opinion is so worded that, at best, only lawyers can comprehend it. . . . There results an esoteric lawyers' jargon. Diplomats have their cant; so, too, do baseball players, physicists and philosophers. Wherefore some legal jargon is inevitable. But we have too much of it. The excess helps keep alive the notion that the springs of decision in judges wholly differ from the springs of decision in other men. It prevents laymen from seeing what judges are doing, prevents them from tuning in.
>
> The publicity given to judicial opinions will, then, remain a good deal of a mockery as long as "law" is regarded as the private possession of a professional guild. This attitude is slowly beginning to break down. It is an idea that should be rejected in toto. The courts should feel obliged to make themselves intelligible to the men on the street or the subway.[50]

Judges seem to have no illusions that they are widely read by laymen and doubt that the public is interested in much of what they write. Evidence based on two interviews with members of the Supreme Court and interviews with other judges and lawyers tends to support this impression. The clear conclusion is that most judges do not expect to be read much by laymen and, therefore, do not think in terms of a lay audience in their writing styles.

Especially bothersome in legal writing, according to Judge Jerome Frank, may be "weasel words" (such as due process) that have deliberately vague meaning. Such terms are often used as if they were precise and clear, thus giving a false impression of continuity, uniformity, and definiteness. There is a tendency to use "holy words" in the form of rules, principles, formulas, and standards that are reduced to "well-polished phrases."[51]

There are meaningful reasons behind much of this ambiguity. Sometimes ambiguity is a device rather than an accident. The Court must function as an institution, which means that for a majority opinion at least five justices must commonly agree on a given statement. They may need to use vague terms that mean one thing to one justice and something else to another, to enable the Court to get rid of the

50. Jerome Frank, *Courts on Trial* (Princeton, N. J.: Princeton University Press, 1949), pp. 258–59.
51. Frank, *Law and the Modern Mind*, pp. 26–27; 57.

case at hand and postpone the problem of precision till a future day that may never come.[52] Compromise in the decision-making process may mean compromise in the decision-wording process. Or, in other words, ambiguities may be a deliberate means of resolving conflict; the real reasons for a decision may be deliberately hidden or masked. In sum:

> Even though the [judicial] opinions open important vistas to us, they are not exactly picture-windows opening onto the Supreme Courtyard. The opinions present only a result, and because the Supreme Court does not deliberate in public, how the result was reached remains cloudy. . . . We see "before" and "after" at the Supreme Court but not "during." . . . When the Justices rise and file out through the drapes . . . behind the bench . . . the curtain literally falls across the Court's proceedings.[53]

Diverse factors go into any attempted further explanation of why the Court's opinion-writing situation is as it is. For example, it can be argued that a justice is supposed to be primarily a thinker and not a writer and thus simply should not be concerned with the art of good writing. Or, it is often pointed out that the nature of the case makes a great difference; some decisions, as in tax fields, would be difficult for even the most skilled writer to make clear.

But perhaps as significant an explanation lies in the concept "feedback"—the return of information and reaction to the source of the message. If the appellate judge is in part a "professional writer," then feedback is important. A writer needs reaction and criticism to develop and improve. But the Supreme Court justice as a writer is isolated. His writing is published whether it is good or bad, and it is given only limited editing in the literary sense of the term.[54]

> No institution in the country more desperately needs critics. A President or a legislator who makes mistakes can be voted out of office, but not a Supreme Court Justice. He is accountable to no one but himself. Nor does he have the freedom of other office-holders to discuss his work with experts in the field. He is alone and immune, and he may

52. John P. Frank, *Marble Palace* (New York: Alfred A. Knopf, 1958), pp. 134–35.

53. Alan F. Westin (ed.), *The Supreme Court: Views From Inside* (New York: W. W. Norton & Co., 1961), p. 6.

54. Leflar, "Some Observations Concerning Judicial Opinions," pp. 815–16.

be peculiarly susceptible to vanity, to basking in the sunshine of his friends' compliments.[55]

In his personal contacts, the justice is seldom exposed to frank criticism on such subjects as writing style. Social gatherings and the cocktail circuit in Washington may lead to general discussions about law, and a justice may even be chided by acquaintances and friends. But he is usually immune to direct criticism on a face-to-face basis because specific details about what is going on at the Court are mostly out of bounds in personal interactions. One result of this shield of social protection is that the justice is left to write pretty much as he pleases. In such an atmosphere, as one expert in law who was interviewed put it, the literary culprit may simply often be "bad habits."

Thus from a communication standpoint, one by-product of this whole decision-making and decision-writing process is that the task of understanding Supreme Court decisions has been made a struggle for both expert and lay consumer long before the Court's decision is ever announced. The conclusion is that the justices themselves tend to be aware of the opinion-writing problem and have tried in recent years to pay more attention to clarity in style. But equally important is the obvious evidence that writing quality still varies from justice to justice and for the same justice over time. In addition, the writing of opinions is considered a very individualistic concern. A justice prides himself on his independence and respects the independence of his colleagues. Thus, writing styles will likely never be stressed as something the whole Court "should work on." The better writers on the Court may set examples, but their degree of influence would seem inherently limited.

THE OPINION RELEASED

Opinion Days: Past and Present

Until the 1965 change from the Monday-only tradition of opinion days, in an October–June term of the Court there might be only fifteen to twenty days when Court decisions would be released. Now, under

55. Anthony Lewis, "The Court and Its Critics," *Minnesota Law Review*, 45 (1960–61): 331–32.

the new system of opinions (usually still announced on Mondays but also sometimes announced on other weekdays), the number of decision days has been roughly doubled.

The main reason for the 1965 change was never officially explained by the Court, but it was clear that the purpose was to avoid the problem of flooding Mondays with numerous decisions especially near the end of each term in June. The spreading out of cases would enable the press to spend more time with most cases.

The Court obviously was hesitant about making the change in the first place, although there are no signs that the Court regrets having made the switch. In fact, interviews around the Court indicate that the new system has generally worked and has been better for most concerned.[56]

Decision Mondays were actually more than just a tradition. Although there is little in print about the practice, it seemingly can be traced back to the nineteenth century.[57] It probably started because Monday was the first day on which decisions could be announced following the Friday (at one time, Saturday) conferences. The system was designed as one means of ensuring secrecy. The weekend allowed time for carefully checking materials with a minimum danger of leaks. But interviews at the Court Building indicate that the new system apparently has not created any serious security problems.

While security was probably the major factor in the Court's hesitancy to change, part of the delay appears to have been simply a resistance to giving in to the demands of the news media. The wire services, the *New York Times*, the *Washington Post*, and others had been urging the Chief Justice for several years to avoid the "dumping" of opinions on the press. *Times* Associate Editor James Reston said that he had talked with Chief Justice Warren in the early 1960's about the problem, but the Chief Justice—while not unsympathetic —had said he did not feel anything could be done.[58] The impression

56. The number of decisions on the final day of each term—usually the most active day of the year for the Court—was cut roughly in half: from 10 to 15 in the 1960/64 period to 7 and 8 in 1965 and 1966. The final 1967 figure, however, jumped back up to 13.

57. *The Docket Sheet* (monthly publication for Supreme Court employees), Vol. 6, No. 4 (April, 1965).

58. Interview with Reston, May 26, 1965.

is that the Court partly resists making any changes for the convenience of newsmen; it does not like to be placed in a position of letting press pressure result in procedural changes.

It is important to stress here several earlier changes in order to gain some historical perspective. The change away from Monday decision days was actually not as major a departure as some changes made earlier. In fact, the Court has not been as inflexible in changing its traditions as some might think; it just takes its time in altering them.

Up until about forty years ago, for example, there were no proofs of opinions available to the press. Newsmen had to write up stories about Court decisions without even having a text of opinions from which to work. Columnist David Lawrence said he had urged Chief Justice William Howard Taft to change this policy, and proofs were finally distributed in the late 1920's.[59] But the press still did not get a copy of the full text until the opinion had been completely read or announced in the courtroom. This policy led to such mistakes as that made in the 1935 Gold Clause cases and to a tendency for the press to make sometimes inaccurate inferences from lengthy opinions.

In the technical and involved Gold Clause cases the Associated Press misinterpreted the majority opinion and transmitted a bulletin stating the opposite of the Court's intent. Byron Price, who was bureau chief at the time, admitted that the AP "made a serious error as a result of too much haste." [60] The error, while soon corrected, could by no means be erased; but it did lead to adoption of the present policy of handing out proofs to newsmen as the justices start to read their opinions in the courtroom. Price outlined what happened after the incident when he contacted Chief Justice Charles Evans Hughes and was invited to the Chief Justice' home on S Street:

> I said I had come on two errands. First of all I had brought an apology for whatever embarrassment had been caused to the Court. Secondly, and without seeking to shift the blame for a bad piece of reporting, I had brought a suggestion which I hoped might minimize the hazards of reporting Supreme Court decisions in the future.
>
> The Chief Justice listened attentively, as he always did, but he manifestly was taken aback when it developed that I was proposing a

59. Interviews with Lawrence, May 25 and May 28, 1965.
60. Personal letter from Price, May 24, 1965.

change in the long established procedure of the Court. What I suggested was that once the reading of an opinion had begun, the entire text be made available to the reporters so that they might see precisely what had been decided. Under that practice, I argued, no reporter would be tempted to speculate in the hope of being first with the news; while on its side the Court, without in any way risking premature disclosure, would save itself from possible confusion over its findings. In summary, I presented the proposal as justified in the interest of the Court, the public, and the press.

Mr. Hughes asked many questions about the physical and technical aspects of the operation I was suggesting. He also dwelt at length on the difficulty of obtaining agreement among the Justices for reversals of procedures so firmly established by long precedent. It was plain, however, that his attitude was becoming more favorable as he turned the question over in his mind. In the end he stated his conclusion: So far as he himself was concerned, he was in total agreement with me. He had to deal, however, with eight tough minded colleagues, as well as precedents, and he was not at all certain his views would prevail. But he would try.

He did try, and succeeded. Shortly thereafter the Court announced that the texts of opinions would be made available henceforth the moment reading from the bench began. . . .[61]

This is still the practice today. The moment the justice starts reading from the bench, newsmen are given the full text of the opinion. Concurring opinions and dissents come later, but the press is able almost immediately to find out how the Court majority decided. Newsmen in the courtroom get the opinions directly. Those in the press room in the basement of the Court Building are given copies by the Press Officer. On decision mornings, the Press Officer has collected all proof (printed) copies of the opinions and has locked them in a cabinet in the press room. When an opinion is released in the courtroom on the first floor, a slip of paper with the case number on it is put into a container and dropped into an air tube; the Press Officer gets the container as it lands at the end of the air tube in the press room. He unlocks the cabinet and starts passing out copies of the just-released decision. This sequence of distribution has become the standard practice at the Court.

Actually, however, another recent change has also affected decision

61. *Ibid.*

days by giving the newsmen more time to report decisions on the day announced. In 1961, the Court changed its meeting time from noon to 10 A.M. But it is hard to determine to what extent this change was made for the sake of the press. Interviews indicate that the primary reason for the shift was that the justices simply preferred the earlier time. (Since 1898, the Court had met from noon until 4:30 P.M., with a half-hour break for lunch at 2 P.M. Court records also show other patterns, such as noon to 4 P.M. with no lunch break [1873–98] and 11 A.M. to 3 P.M. with no lunch break [1808–72].)

The Court at various times has considered other changes in opinion-day procedures and the release of opinions to the news media and the public. Several of these considerations will be examined later but, in general, it seems clear that the Court has been reluctant to give up most of its current opinion-releasing practices. Preoccupation with security makes it unlikely that major changes in the Court's traditional ways of operating will be made. In particular, fear of leaks that might affect the economy is probably the main factor preventing any advance release of information.[62]

Oral Announcement of Decisions

One tradition that the Court has considered doing away with is the oral announcement of opinions; but although the practice is periodically reconsidered, it appears likely to continue as an established part of Court procedure—at least in the near future.

As some legal scholars have observed, there is considerable anachronism in the tradition. It would seem the busy Court is interrupting its pressing work to tell a few persons in the courtroom what has happened. It is, indeed, ironic that most of those in the courtroom do not learn the final outcome of a major decision as quickly as a person might in, say, Los Angeles. While a major decision is being read by a justice, the result is flashed across the country by the news services in a matter of minutes. The several hundred visitors in the courtroom may be among the last to know.

62. A conclusion reinforced by Gilbert Cranberg, "The Court and Its Public: Warren's View," *Des Moines Register,* Oct. 16, 1966; "What Did the Supreme Court Say?" *Saturday Review,* April 8, 1967, pp. 90–92.

The oral announcement is not the official act that "makes" a decision; Court opinions would become official without oral delivery because, Court staff believe, the opinion is only "of record" once it has been filed with the Clerk of the Court with the Chief Justice' signature on it. In theory, then, a decision does not become official at the time of the oral announcement of the opinion; in practice, however, this reading of the opinion is considered more than just a gesture. It is the moment when justices feel their opinions have been formally released for all to hear. In fact, this symbolic act of commitment in public is apparently one major reason why the practice is continued. The tradition does have meaning.

Supporters of oral announcements of decisions also see the traditional ceremony as a chance for visitors to the Court Building to hear "history being made." And the practice serves to tell directly those parties in the case (who often are in the courtroom) what has happened. For those interested in a specific case or the Court in general, the ceremony often can be deeply gratifying.

But such is not always the case, at least from the standpoint of satisfying curiosity about exactly what the Court has decided. In fact, it may be very hard for a person not familiar with a case to understand the oral announcement. The first-time visitor to the courtroom may be so overpowered by the surroundings as to be distracted from the real action. In addition, if the case is complicated, even a clear summary is left fuzzy unless the listener is well informed on the case. Often what is needed most is a chance to read and reread carefully the justices' words.

Many times a justice simply reads excerpts from his opinion; at other times he will summarize and paraphrase. The differences between the written opinion and oral announcement are usually slight, but close observers of the Court often find the courtroom commentary especially revealing. Sometimes the oral announcement tells more about the way a justice feels than does his written opinion. The written word cannot convey strong emotion that may be evident.

Justice Hugo Black, in particular, may add meaningful color and interpretation to his opinions. A significant example here is his 1962 school prayer opinion in which he made the extemporaneous remark that "The prayer of each man from his soul must be his and his alone. . . ." [63] Observers on that decision day noted that Justice Black read his majority school prayer opinion with considerable emotion. Some argue that anyone who could have heard the justice's remarks in person would never have been confused into thinking that the justice was anti-religious.

Although the written opinion of the Court is all that technically counts for the development of the law, there are on occasion significant happenings during oral announcements. In 1963, in *Arizona v. California*, for example:

> As [Justice] Douglas read on [in dissent], his face, always ruddy, flushed and his voice began to bristle. "The decision," he said, ". . . has made the dream of the federal bureaucracy come true by granting it, for the first time, the life-and-death power of dispensation of water rights."
> There was a heightening of attention in the courtroom as Douglas read. The sharp words, the tone of voice, were unlike him. His anger was aroused and on public display as it had seldom been in recent years.[64]

Sometimes there will be clashes among specific members of the Court. In 1959, Justice Douglas criticized Justice Whittaker for a "smart-alecky" opinion; and in 1962, Chief Justice Warren got annoyed when Justice Frankfurter added extemporaneously: "I know what the Court has said but I don't understand the meaning of it." The Chief Justice' reaction was to snap back with a restatement of his view of the case.[65]

Newsmen who cover the Court without spending much time in the courtroom during oral announcements assume such "exciting" moments are so few as not to be worth worrying about. But sometimes the unexpected happens and hearing the oral announcement gives a newsman further insights into judicial thinking. Sometimes, indeed, there are minor differences between the written opinion and the oral announcement. Justice Frankfurter, for example, who always appeared to speak without notes, often delivered an opinion that sounded unlike his written opinion, although it basically meant the same thing.

63. Quoted in the *New York Times*, June 26, 1962.
64. Clayton, *The Making of Justice*, p. 252.
65. *Ibid.*, pp. 103–4.

So even though it is the written formal opinions that become law, the oral announcement is often significant for the newsman who is trying to get at exactly what was decided by the Court, how, and why. For the newsman under deadline pressure who needs to be near a telephone in the Court press room, the problem of trying to be in two places at the same time is just another of the major obstacles faced in trying to communicate Supreme Court decisions.

III
The Press

COMPARISON WITH OTHER NEWS SETTINGS

THE PRESS CORPS throughout Washington enjoys both prestige and special privileges.[1] Although coverage at the Court is similar in some ways to other governmental news work in Washington, there are differences that make the job especially demanding and, sometimes, especially restrictive and frustrating.

"Fast reading, clear thinking, familiarity with procedures and steady nerves are prerequisites of the job." [2] Although helpful, such a description of the Court news assignment goes only part way in pinpointing the unusual elements. More specifically, for example, the Court newsman has to have a perceptive and analytical mind; in contrast to a reporter covering most other government news beats, he does not need much aggressiveness and doggedness in his approach.[3]

The Court job in many ways is like no other in Washington. The Court is the only part of the federal government where the newsman is left totally on his own. There are no officials available for consultation during the moments after a decision is announced. There

1. Douglass Cater, *The Fourth Branch of Government* (Boston: Houghton Mifflin Co., 1959), p. 1.
2. Earl Johnson, *U.P.I. Reporter*, Jan. 25, 1962.
3. Interview with James Clayton, March 12, 1965.

43

are no press conferences or briefings. One of the staples of the reporter's way of life—the interview—is, for all practical purposes, nonexistent. The newsman has only his background knowledge, notes, typewriter, desk, and phone—and whatever resources or contacts they can provide as he hastens to call in his story or to get down on paper what the Court has decided.

Much of the job involves building up a backlog of written and nonrecorded data on cases the Court could hand down. Except for the final decision day of each term, the newsman never knows for certain which cases he will have to write about. The task of a decision day has been described as "taking an open-book exam in Constitutional Law." [4]

There is one overriding difference between Supreme Court coverage and other types which is not readily apparent. In many news fields, there is at least partial truth in the statement that if the press has not covered a news development, the event or trend, in effect, has not "happened." [5] News is what the press makes it; the press by its selection of events to report, in a sense, "makes" the event happen; many things are "real" only if the press has reported them.

By contrast, each case before the Court goes into history books whether or not the press has written a word on it. There is an automatic and permanent record on everything the Court has decided which, in effect, acts as a check on the newsman covering the Court. A missed case, improper emphasis, or an error in fact in a news story will be obvious for those experts in the field who have a chance to read exactly what the Court said. By comparison, in other news fields, many public officials (such as in Congress or the State Department) have to rely heavily on the press for interpretation and information. They may be fairly sure when the press is right or wrong, but seldom is an entire record laid out so clearly. In addition, there is the possibility that someone else knows something that the public official does not know. Thus he is forced partly to trust the press because

4. Dana Bullen of the *Washington Evening Star*, quoted by Caryl Rivers, "Lawyer Prefers Reporting to Arguing of Big Issues," *Editor & Publisher*, Aug. 8, 1964, p. 42.

5. Bernard C. Cohen, *The Press and Foreign Policy* (Princeton, N. J.: Princeton University Press, 1963), p. 13.

his own sources of information may be incomplete or only impressionistic.[6]

This reliance (or lack of it) has an important effect on the newsman–news-source relationship. Because of the formal Court record, the lawyer and the lower court judge do not "need" the news media. They can ignore the media and still find out nearly all that has happened by reading the written opinions. The law is often a slow process; the lawyer or judge can usually afford to wait to see the full record in legal journals and volumes of cases. The law is there and can wait until it is needed. There is no other area of government where the whole record is laid out as conveniently in one place. Even the *Congressional Record* does not give as complete a view of legislative activity.

Thus, the situation for the Court newsman is unique because, in theory, anyone interested has access to most of the same sources that the news reporter has. In contrast to other areas of news work, the Supreme Court reporter operates with few special advantages or facilities, few special means of access to personal sources, and few special materials or documents.

Indeed, the physical setting in the Court Building affects how the newsman will go about covering the Court. For example, as noted in the last chapter, there is the obvious problem of needing to be in the main-floor courtroom during oral announcements of opinions while the phones and typewriters are in the basement press room. (The main press room includes several tables, desks, and typewriters, three phone booths, and several cubicles. In a nearby room down the hall are two other desks for newsmen. These niches and facilities are for use mostly by the "regulars"—or most active—reporters: especially by those from the two wire services—Associated Press and United Press International—and from the *New York Times, Washington Post,* and *Washington Evening Star.*)

The main press room has space for the twenty or twenty-five reporters who are often or occasionally around the Court, such as those for the *Wall Street Journal*, Newhouse National News Service,

6. Besides Cohen, among other sources especially helpful here was Donald R. Matthews, *U.S. Senators and Their World* (Chapel Hill, N. C.: University of North Carolina Press, 1960).

Baltimore Sun, or *Time.* Although on a busy day thirty or forty news-men may be covering the Court, the press room is usually big enough to hold the crowd. One reason is that some of the regular reporters are in the courtroom throughout the oral announcements; it is not usual-ly until all the opinions have been announced that the press room becomes flooded. Also, the wire services usually have one or two of their staff in the special separate booths beneath the courtroom. The proof copies of decisions are stuffed in containers and sped down-stairs to these booths (via the air tube) by another staff member stationed in the courtroom. The news stories are then filed directly from these booths.

Facilities in the courtroom itself include several desks right in front of the justices' bench. These are primarily for the regular news reporters and their assistants. Other reporters have space provided along one side of the courtroom in what might best be described as "the wings." These facilities are not unlike box seats at the theater, but the main difference is that each section is jammed with nine or so straight-backed chairs. A total of perhaps thirty newsmen can be squeezed into these areas, although a comfortable figure would be only ten or twelve. There is a writing ledge for the six or so in front row seats. A public address system from the bench helps newsmen and spectators hear the justices and oral arguments by attorneys. But those far from the bench can only hear clearly if the system is turned up high enough and if the justices remember to (or want to) use the microphones in front of them.

The situation at the Court and the Court's philosophy toward press relations are reflected especially in the role of the Press Officer. While press relations personnel are important in the newsman's day-to-day operation in most governmental fields, the Supreme Court Press Of-ficer is of little real importance for newsmen. He is primarily a feeder of information, not a source. His job is primarily to disseminate materials—not ideas, explanations, or background information on judicial reasoning. Most courts have nothing even approaching a press official and the very existence of the job reflects a concern for the un-usual situation. But, still, the job of Supreme Court Press Officer is severely restricted in scope. He is in no way a spokesman for the Court.

Since 1947, the job has been held by Banning (Bert) Whittington, who previously had covered the Court for United Press. His job is basically to help the press on decision days by handing out opinions and to maintain the facilities at other times. He and his one secretary answer newsmen's queries by phone or in person, but they usually restrict their answers to such matters as whether a certain opinion has been handed down, when the Court will meet next, or what cases are scheduled to be argued.

The Press Officer is usually not hounded with questions by veterans around the building. Even new arrivals soon find they often will get no more than a "perhaps" or "maybe" or "don't know" response. The Press Officer seldom discusses specifics about cases; he gives no attempt at interpretation and seldom attempts to clarify issues or to answer questions that might involve opinion or judgment.

In analyzing the Press Officer's job it is difficult to distinguish between what is attributable to the individual and what is inherent in his role. The Press Officer's assignment is largely determined by others; he has virtually no power or policy-making function. As a staff member of the Court, he is responsible to the Chief Justice. The result is that he is usually closemouthed about everything. His view is that the Court does not and should not give the press much help— that the institution is a Court of law, not a legislature.[7]

Perhaps the best example of the Press Officer's role can be found in a memo tacked to the press room bulletin board for several years. Dated Oct. 10, 1963, and signed by Whittington, the notice reminded newsmen that: there are only a limited number of opinion proofs available for distribution to the press; priority for copies is given to regulars at the Court; and no proofs are guaranteed to anyone unless the newsman subscribes to a Government Printing Office service. The point is clear: the press room is run largely on a "first-come" basis. Newsmen are accepted but not courted.

Another example of this philosophy at work came when the Monday-only, opinion-day policy was changed in April, 1965. No reason for the change was stated officially by the Court. When asked a few questions by newsmen, the Press Officer made a call or two around the Court Building but made no special effort to give a firm answer. The press was left to infer the reason for the change and

7. Interview with Whittington, May 6, 1965.

thus was somewhat in doubt. By not providing information, the Press Officer helped "protect" the Court. In a sense, he is a spokesman by his silence: "The Court has nothing to say."

Personal Interaction with the Justices

Law is a step-by-step, often slow process, working on the principle of modification rather than sudden revision.[8] By contrast with much news media work—that which looks for the sudden, the dramatic, the quickly gathered—it is not surprising that certain tensions and an incompatibility between judges and newsmen should exist. There is a basic conflict in objectives. Such conflict between the journalist and the government official is not necessarily irreconcilable, but it does lead to an uneasy relationship and different definitions as to what is news.

It is not surprising to find an ambivalent "love-hate" type of relationship on the part of public officials toward the press. The newsman is in control of much of the information flow—a position which, along with economic backing of a mass news medium, provides considerable power.[9] Included is a kind of "threatening power" which sometimes derives from fear and uncertainty on the part of many news sources.

As with other governmental officials, many judges acquire at least some awareness of the public through the mass media. But instead of saying that the Court follows the press closely, it would be more appropriate to say that the justices tend to follow public opinion closely through the press. It is clear that news media comment and public reaction cannot be easily separated but that it is usually the latter that judges are more interested in.

Any talk about press influence on the Court should stress the clear pattern of the Eastern media establishment—the *New York Times*, *Washington Post*, *Washington Evening Star*, *Wall Street Journal*, and *Time-Life*. The justices' exposure is primarily an Eastern exposure. There is some truth in the view that for many in Washington the rest of the United States does not seem to exist. While the judge in

8. Walter F. Murphy and C. Herman Pritchett. *Courts, Judges, and Politics* (New York: Random House, 1961), pp. 126–27.
9. See Cohen, *The Press and Foreign Policy*.

Boise, Idaho, may be isolated, his counterpart in Washington, D.C., may be insulated.

But even with such publications as the *Times* and *Post*, there does not seem to be great attention to editorial commentary. In fact, there is still considerable truth in the observation made by Max Freedman in 1956:

> The judges of the Supreme Court do not care what is said about them in the press. A judge may be ruffled for an hour or two by some indignant blast from somebody's editorial page but basically the Court is indifferent because it feels that the editor has failed to pay the intellectual dues of hard work which should precede the right to an opinion.[10]

The important point in this interaction situation, then, is that an individual justice' relations with newsmen may depend largely on his general attitude toward the press and toward specific news organizations. In such a framework, *New York Times* and *Washington Post* reporters and columnists simply tend to be favored most by the Court.

Significantly, much of any justice' interest in the press has been centered on questions of the quality of the news coverage. The justices are obviously aware of the problem of the press in covering the Court, although their means of expressing concern and their attitudes toward this problem vary greatly.

Besides the cautious concern expressed by Chief Justice Warren about lack of public understanding, at least five other members of the recent Court have spoken or written about the problems of Court coverage and public understanding. Chief Justice Warren's view has been that the Court is inadequately covered by the media—partly because much of the reporting is hampered by the traditional interest in treating the Court as a source of spot news and headlines without relevance to the principles at issue.[11] Three justices—Tom C. Clark, John M. Harlan, and William O. Douglas—have been specific in their criticism of press coverage.[12] Justice William J. Brennan, Jr.,

10. Max Freedman, "Worst Reported Institution," *Nieman Reports.* 10(April, 1956): 2.

11. Gilbert Cranberg, "What Did the Supreme Court Say?" *Saturday Review,* April 8, 1967, p. 92. Also: *Report of Committees,* 1966 annual meeting of the Association of American Law Schools, pp. 331-32.

12. From a variety of sources, mostly speeches. A general list of relevant references can be found in the Bibliography under each justice' name.

has included the press in his general expressions of concern about misunderstandings of the Court. Perhaps the most involved critic of all was Felix Frankfurter, who played several significant, behind-the-scenes roles in calling attention to press coverage problems and in urging others to do something about them.

There are a few elements of historical perspective that should be stressed here. Although most of the concern expressed by justices about press coverage has come in recent years, as far back as 1944, Chief Justice Harlan F. Stone said he was "really shocked" by the "misleading, not to say completely inaccurate, statements" about Supreme Court decisions in the press.[13] His concern was probably a major factor in the Chief Justice' tense relationship with newsmen. But perhaps as important was the fact that he "liked to talk"—with the result that some of his candid remarks ended up in print. Over time he became sensitive to the fact that he had ended up in trouble because of what newsmen had written.[14] (The same problem apparently bothered Chief Justice William Howard Taft, who on occasion hesitantly granted interviews with newsmen and then generally was plagued by such off-hand remarks.)[15]

Historically, perhaps the single most significant incident in establishing press relations may have involved Chief Justice John Marshall. In 1819, Chief Justice Marshall broke his usual public silence by writing anonymous articles in defense of *McCulloch* v. *Maryland,* These appeared in the *Philadelphia Union,* April 28 and May 1, 1819, but the experience was so unhappy that he seldom spoke up in print again:

Once the articles appeared, Marshall had second thoughts about them.

> He told Justice Story that he did not want them reprinted in New England; he felt that the meaning had been distorted by the printer (who had rearranged some parts), so that the argument was now "mangled and unclear." Marshall was also worried about the articles being traced back to him, and refused to allow them to be published

13. Quoted in Alpheus T. Mason, *Harlan Fiske Stone, Pillar of the Law* (New York: Viking Press, 1956), p. 626.

14. *Ibid.*, pp. 699–700.

15. Alpheus T. Mason, *William Howard Taft: Chief Justice* (New York: Simon & Schuster, 1965), pp. 278–79.

by Henry Wheaton, the Reporter of the Court's decisions, in the Appendix to the official volume of the year's opinions.[16]

Chief Justice Marshall's stature in the development of the law and Supreme Court may not have been crucial here, but one can guess that the Chief Justice' eventual policies with the press and his feelings about public commentary may have set much of the precedent for later silence by the Court.

Members of today's Court, however, do have considerable contact with newsmen in their chambers, by phone, and at other official and social gatherings. In fact, there has been a bit more personal inter-action behind the scenes than one might expect, although the judges, of course, restrict themselves in what they say.

Discussion of Court topics, almost without exception, is limited. Interviews by justices are granted, but not often, and the subject matter is restricted to general issues; there is little or no discussion of specific cases, although evidence is that silence surrounding a case may be eased somewhat after the decision is announced.

When personal meetings are held, the sessions are nearly always for background purposes only—meaning that there may be no attribution of comments as coming from a member of the Court. The policy is similar to, but stricter than, many "off-the-record" sessions held elsewhere in the nation's Capital. Here, there is little chance to attribute such interview comments to a vague "Court observer" or to a "top level federal appellate judge."

Thus, much of the interchange between justice and newsman is confined to private and "non-newsy" interaction. Or, as another example, after a decision has been handed down, newsmen have on occasion found a note from a member of the Court saying something to the effect, "You didn't read page 6 of my opinion." Occasionally at social gatherings, a justice may make a similar passing remark to a newsman or indicate something about a news report or point out a certain case that might be interesting to read. Such social gatherings allow for some general discussion of law or newspaper work. But in contrast to other areas of government, the cocktail party is not considered a time when news items about the Court are to leak

16. Alan F. Westin (ed.), *An Autobiography of the Supreme Court* (New York: Macmillan Co., 1963), pp. 77–78.

out. At many legislative or executive branch gatherings, public officials often play the game of "planting" news items with the journalist seeking out talkative souls. But although the justices may relax their guards, there is no game being played. The party is not a time for the journalist to try to break down the firm barrier of secretiveness surrounding the justices.

However, it is also important to note historical exceptions to this barrier. Fred Starek, Cincinnati newspaperman and politician, was a good friend of Chief Justice Taft and was involved in correspondence with Taft concerning the possible appointment of Stone as Chief Justice. Irving Brant, newsman and author, was an influence in some of President Franklin Roosevelt's judicial appointments. And Chief Justice Salmon P. Chase was "very willing to win an ally in the press who would tell his story as he wished it to be read." Also, Chief Justice Stone, in his early years on the bench, was sometimes able to persuade friends to write articles for publication, thus, in effect, planting favorable articles in legal or other publications.[17]

In recent years, probably the most active justice in relations with the press has been Felix Frankfurter. His influence and involvement was often indirect and very much behind the scenes.[18] Specifically, one of Justice Frankfurter's friends was James Reston of the *New York Times*. In fact, it was his relationship with Reston that helped launch the *Times*'s policy of using Supreme Court newsmen trained in law. The success of the *Times* venture then led, in part, to the adoption of a similar policy by the *Washington Post* and others.

Reston confirms that it was Justice Frankfurter who first urged the *Times* to have a man trained in the law.[19] He recalls that the justice once remarked to him personally in the mid–1950's that the *Times* would not think of sending a sports reporter to Yankee Stadium who knew as little about baseball as *Times* reporters knew about

17. From Mason, *William Howard Taft*, p. 297; Samuel Krislov, *The Supreme Court in the Political Process* (New York: Macmillan Co., 1965), p. 17; Henry Adams, *The Education of Henry Adams* (Boston: Houghton Mifflin Co., 1918), p. 250; and Mason, *Harlan Fiske Stone*, p. 303.

18. For example, Law Professor Philip B. Kurland, a critic of Court press coverage, said his awareness of the problem came largely as the result of his clerkships with Justice Frankfurter and Judge Jerome Frank. (Personal interview with Professor Kurland, Washington, D.C., May 19, 1965.)

19. Personal interview, May 26, 1965.

the Court. Reston is unsure exactly what happened after that but recollects that Anthony Lewis was hired with the expectation that he would get training in law. Lewis confirms that he was hired with the understanding that he would go to law school for a year before settling firmly on the Court beat.[20]

The relationship between Justice Frankfurter and Lewis turned out to be unusual. There still are rumors around the Court Building that Lewis was able to get "inside" information from the justice that other reporters did not get—especially background information on cases and trends. Lewis firmly denies any such relationship: "It never happened and could not have. The rumors may have stemmed from the fact that he had, as you know, a general interest in my career." [21]

Former staff personnel for the justice doubt that any unusual information was exchanged between Lewis and him. One former staff member said that Justice Frankfurter used to give "stern lectures" about the "unusual prevalence of information seekers in Washington," making it clear that he would fire anyone on the spot who handed out tips about cases.

At the same time, however, the unique friendship between Justice Frankfurter and Lewis must be acknowledged. They did on occasion have lunch together in the justice' chambers and did have a few personal social meetings away from the Court Building. It is clear that Lewis probably had more access to justices and other Court and government personnel than did any newsman in Court history.

The Newsman's Reaction to His Role

It is especially intriguing to analyze the reaction of the press to such a restrictive news environment. Indeed, several patterns of news-gathering and news-writing behavior become clear.

Instead of being active and aggressive searchers of news and interpretation, many Court newsmen have tended to be passive. Here an obvious element of role reversal exists—a switch from the searching-

20. Letter dated May 18, 1965.
21. Letter dated June 4, 1965. It is especially interesting that Justice Frankfurter once said of Lewis: "There are not two members of the Court itself who could get the gist of each decision so accurately in so few words." Cited in William L. Rivers, *The Opinionmakers* (Boston: Beacon Press, 1965), p. 89.

out approach of news-gathering to a somewhat sit-back-with-the-feet-up approach. Newsmen also have shown considerable deference to the institution—with many admitting their deep respect for or even awe of the Court. Absent is that feeling of mutual distrust often evidenced between the press and lower branches of the judiciary.

Newsmen around the Court Building do criticize the justices, but much of this type of reaction is limited to complaints about how the justices write opinions.[22] Even doubts (many of which may be valid) about judicial inconsistencies, unsupported reasoning, lack of clearly defined legal boundaries, or internal squabblings among justices are barely expressed. Judicial reasoning and the wisdom of decisions are seldom attacked—either publicly or privately. This generally accepting philosophy of the press, of course, is in marked contrast to relationships existing between the news corps and many other news sources in Washington. Policy decisions are constantly under scrutiny in most areas of government, but Court newsmen give little evidence that they see themselves in such a "watchdog" role. There is, as a result, little overt friction between justice and newsman—at least not to the extent often evidenced between the press and presidents or congressmen.

There are several obvious and not-so-obvious reasons why newsmen have tended to react passively to the news situation they are in. One explanation, of course, is that the Court is somewhat awe-inspiring. Indeed, the law and the justices and the Court Building are all cloaked with that "mystique and divinity"—at least for many a newcomer. And, too, the complexity of the law forces the journalist to be humble; the Court beat simply cannot be mastered in the way a reporter might learn to work with his news sources at the United States Census Bureau or on a House appropriations subcommittee.

22. If a popularity poll of recent Courts were taken among newsmen, the justice who would be most criticized for his writing would probably be Frankfurter. Among other "more difficult" writers would be Justices White and Harlan. Those usually found easiest to read would include Justice Clark, Chief Justice Warren, Justice Black, and perhaps Justice Douglas. (Although Justice Douglas is probably the best "writer" on the Court, some reporters admit they find his legal opinions—while "colorful" and "easy to read"—sometimes uncomfortably inconsistent with his earlier opinions or too vague and sweeping in language. There is often an uneasiness that the words used and his real meaning or feelings may not be quite the same.)

But perhaps an even more crucial reason for this deference and passivity is the fact that the Court press corps probably has less power and influence than any other major news group in Washington. In contrast to the "fourth estate" and the "participating" congressional and White House reporters, even the acknowledged leaders in Court press coverage influence little, if anything, that the Court decides.[23] The press does affect the public image of what the Court has said, but there is little evidence of anything more than this role of transmission of information and understanding.

Still another explanation may be found by comparing the situation at the Supreme Court with the role of the press at other court levels. Lower court judges, including those at the important United States Courts of Appeals, tend to be more accessible to newsmen and tend to talk more about finished cases. They even may try to explain the legal reasoning of a case.[24] The single overriding reason for less accessibility at the Supreme Court level is simply that the Court is considered unique. As one lower court judge observed, the "risks" seem greater at the Supreme Court. Newsmen interviewed tended to agree. Indeed, newsmen as well as others feel that, because the Supreme Court is so special, interviewing which might seem proper at lower courts is not necessarily acceptable at the highest court.

Perhaps the best evidence of all such deference can be found in the minor—but still significant—news event created by the Court's April, 1965, announcement of a change in Monday-only opinion days. After the announcement was made, newsmen around the press room were inquisitive, and a few asked "Why?" But they did not push the point. Absent was any attempt to find out firmly the reasons for the change or to learn how permanent it was meant to be. Most of the press were content to report that "apparently" the change was made to avoid the problem of flooding the media with too many opinions. But the "why" of the news story was never pinned down; the Court was allowed to speak without being pressed for reasons or clarifica-

23. Among the many sources on Washington press "power," see especially: Cater, *The Fourth Branch of Government*; Cohen, *The Press and Foreign Policy*; Rivers, *The Opinionmakers*; and Matthews, *U. S. Senators and Their World*.

24. Based on interviews with federal and state appellate judges and newsmen covering federal and state appellate courts.

tion. The analytical point here is not to judge whether such a non-aggressive approach is good or bad but simply to point out that newsmen in other parts of Washington would not have tended so easily to sit back; or, at least, they would have stressed the Court's refusal or reluctance to comment. It is not only important to note that there are few sources of information around the Court; it is also significant that many newsmen do not rigorously explore the few channels that are open or seek out new ones.

A Case Study in Decision-making under Deadline Pressure[25]

> Except on the psychiatrist's couch, the flow of mental images has not been extensively used in research. The simple instrument of asking respondents to name who or what had just come into their minds, while obvious in the light of its use in psychiatry, has not been in the standard battery of techniques of behavioral science research. Perhaps one reason has been that the content of free associations seemed relatively inaccessible to careful experimentation. A subject's report of his associations cannot be independently validated, and he has so many obvious motivations for distorting them. We have no illusions that the reports of free associations . . . are either very reliable or complete . . . however . . . a portion of the image flow can be recaptured.[26]

In the de Sola Pool and Shulman study, reporters were interviewed right after writing news stories. Although the methods used were preferable to earlier ones, more insight could be gained if we could get even closer to the newsman's thinking process.[27] But the problem then becomes how to avoid interfering with a newsman at work while trying to get close enough to watch him in action.

25. The following section is basically an extension and slightly revised version of the author's, "Decision-Making by a Reporter Under Deadline Pressure," *Journalism Quarterly*, 43(Autumn, 1966): 419–28.

26. Ithiel de Sola Pool and Irwin Shulman, "Newsmen's Fantasies, Audiences, and Newswriting," *Public Opinion Quarterly*, 23 (1959): 158.

27. The "pioneer" study in observing newsmen at work was David M. White, "The 'Gate Keeper': A Case Study in the Selection of News," *Journalism Quarterly*, 27 (1950): 383–90. For a fuller recent list of other studies in the gatekeeper area, see Eugene J. Webb and Jerry R. Salancik, "Notes on the Sociology of Knowledge," *Journalism Quarterly*, 42(1965):595–96.

Fortunately, an especially good opportunity arose to watch a Court newsman at work. The newsman-observation analysis recorded below shows in specific detail the setting and conditions under which a reporter at the Court has to work and captures some of the more general decision-making problems involved in assembling and writing a news story.

Method and Procedure

Dana Bullen, Court reporter for the *Washington Evening Star*, was selected as the subject of this observation for several reasons:

1) The job for the *Star* reflects, in a sense, a compromise between both wire service- and *New York Times*-type philosophies of covering the Court. As an afternoon paper, the *Star* must emphasize speed (as do the wire services); but, at the same time, the *Star* seeks (as does the *Times* or *Washington Post*) to provide fairly detailed, interpretative coverage of the Court.

2) It seemed likely that Bullen would not be much affected by someone looking over his shoulder. As a (then) thirty-three-year-old bachelor and ex-Marine, Bullen had an air of self-confidence and assurance. His background included a B.A. in journalism and a law degree, both from the University of Florida; he received a 1964 award from the American Bar Association for his Court coverage—an honor given to only a few newsmen at the Court over the years. He also was awarded a Nieman Fellowship at Harvard University for the 1966/67 academic year to study constitutional law, in particular.

3) The facilities where Bullen works are somewhat isolated. He shares the small office near the press room with one of the wire service reporters, but this reporter is usually working elsewhere when opinions are being handed down. Because of this it was possible to watch Bullen work at his desk with few other newsmen around, thus avoiding some biases which might stem from the social pressure of colleagues.

There were other advantages in the physical arrangement. Because the *Star* is an afternoon paper, much of Bullen's work must be done quickly by dictating stories over the phone and by talking with his editors on the national news desk. Much of what he does can be captured simply by listening.[28]

Bullen was in a working situation where it would be hard to interfere with anything that he was doing. Despite his awareness that he was being watched and his normal urge to "look good," Bullen's over-all reaction to the observation was that the situation had not changed his general behavior much, if at all. He simply felt too busy with real deadlines to be worried about much else.

This single case study, of course, cannot be considered representative of all news work at the Court. It is limited to a description of the effort of one man on one fairly typical decision day and an analysis of his process of making news judgments.[29]

Results: The Diary, May 24, 1965

The following minute-by-minute account records highlights in summary form. Data collected here is a combination of research observations, the writing down of Bullen's telephone conversations, and statements by Bullen to the observer as to what he was doing or thinking about. In several situations, clarification or amplification of behavior was obtained during a brief post-observation discussion between the researcher and Bullen.

By this day in May there were about fifteen cases left of the more than 150 that the Court was to rule on during the 1964/65 term. In addition there were numerous Court orders pending (on whether the Court would hear or deny review of lower court decisions). With a couple of decision days still likely to be left in the term, the justices were expected to announce anywhere from one or two to perhaps more than half a dozen of the remaining decisions. Bullen faced three deadlines for the *Star's* main editions at the time: 10:55 A.M.

28. In addition, the room layout was especially helpful. A chair to the left of Bullen's desk provided a good obervation point, especially when he was hardest at work. He would swing a bit to his right—thus leaving the observer out of his line of vision and literally looking over his shoulder.

29. For other details on methodological problems, see "Decision-Making by Reporter Under Deadline Pressure," especially pp. 420–21. A practice run-through was held the week before (May 17). No significant differences between the May 17 and May 24 sessions were noted except that the former turned out to be a "very light" news day. Fortunately, May 24 turned out to be fairly close to what he called average or typical.

(main area edition); 12:15 P.M. (primarily home delivery); and 1:25 P.M. (primarily street sales).

The justices were to convene at 10 A.M. sharp. Bullen entered the Court Building about 9:15 A.M. and went directly to the cafeteria in the basement for breakfast.

9:38 A.M.—Bullen enters his basement office. He has just found out from the Press Officer that there are 175 lawyers to be sworn in, a ritual which will take easily a half hour. He sees red light attached to his phone that means office has called while he was away.

9:40—Calls office. No one has yet been assigned to cover special ceremony for former Justice Burton, who recently died. Former President Truman is not coming, which takes some of the edge off the occasion. Asks how manpower situation is and lets it be known that he has busy day. Situation left that someone else will cover the ceremony.

9:42—Calls national news desk and tells editor that there are 175 lawyers being admitted to practice, including a Catholic nun. Says he assumes one of the wire services is following up on the nun. Matters left that way.

9:45—Takes off suit coat and sits back in swivel chair. Starts reading the morning *Washington Post*. Flips and scans pages.

9:47—Sees article on [then] Justice Goldberg speaking at a Unitarian church. Tears article from paper.

9:50—Throws *Post* into nearby wastebasket and starts skimming the *New York Times*. Wants to make sure nothing has happened that might affect a Court story—such as Billie Sol Estes out on bail at the time his case before the Court might be announced.

9:51—Tears out Fred Graham story from San Juan, Puerto Rico, on bar meeting and tosses onto desk with other article.

9:52—Tears out small "personal item" and stuffs in shirt pocket.

9:53—Rips out story on false arrests in New York. Might be worth checking locally some time. Tears out article on antitrust action in bank mergers.

9:54—Throws *Times* into wastebasket.

9:55—Several newsmen from wire service (with whom he shares office) enter room—one is photographer who wants to get picture of the nun with her sponsor, Senator Hart from Michigan. The five-minute warning buzzer sounds.

9:56—Leaves office with pencils for sharpening to see if he can "find out any clues."

9:57—Returns with sharpened pencils. Press Officer still out getting the stack of written opinions.

9:58—Leaves for washroom. Wire service men leave. Room now empty.

10:02—Press Officer wheels opinions down hall on cart to Press Room near Bullen's office. Bullen re-enters office. Has been told by Press Officer there may be "one good one." Starts thinking in terms of Billie Sol Estes case (on television in Texas courtroom) or birth control case (on ban of birth control clinic in Connecticut).

10:03—Decides not to call office yet. Pulls out folders and starts sorting through file on Estes. Folder consists of twenty–twenty-five sheets of paper with clippings attached, plus typed and penciled notes. Several paragraphs of background material are marked boldly alongside clippings of earlier story. These could be used again— "lifted out" nearly verbatim, if necessary. Starts to skim pages, looking for the main ideas, occasionally marking sections with large crosses or stars.

10:07—Starts to look at birth control story folder. This consists of fifteen–twenty pages. Makes special note with red pencil that law is eighty-six years old. Comes across background memorandum of case prepared by the Association of American Law Schools. Memo is heavily underlined and is skipped over. "Too late if don't know now."

10:10—Turns to folder on antitrust cases. Bullen's reaction: these are complicated.

10:12—Continues skimming the four–five pages, again marking stars with red pencil next to the passages.

10:15—Looks at a labor case.

10:16—Looks at a case on Communists in labor union offices.

10:17—Looks at case involving destroying of Communist mail by the Post Office. Briefs had been read earlier; skimming used here as a "refresher process."

10:18—A *Star* business page reporter enters room, says hello, heads for couch, and sits down with a copy of the *Times*. Bullen comments that there may be only three or four opinions and that it's uncertain if there will be any stories for business page reporter to handle. Reporter nods and continues reading.

10:19—Bullen gets up and walks to cabinet to check wire service file of briefs on Communist mail case. (There are three full sets of briefs—one for the Associated Press, one for the United Press International, and one for all the other Court newsmen. The file in the office is handy and is used fairly often—with permission.) Checks name of propaganda publication involved.

10:20—Returns to desk.

10:23—Looks at folder on natural gas rate cases.

10:24—Goes out of room "to see what's happening."

10:25—Returns to office, sits down, and leans back in chair.

10:27—Gives copy of resolution honoring Justice Burton to business page reporter—pointing out that it is self-explanatory.

10:28—Looks up at wall clock and notes that the 10:55 deadline nears. Looks out window and continues to lean back in chair.

10:31—Gets up suddenly and goes out of office. The business page reporter continues to read the resolution honoring Justice Burton.

10:33—Bullen returns, hands file on Justice Burton to business page reporter. Says photographer will be in for the 11 A.M. ceremony. Does other reporter want to stay around? Yes. It's agreed.

10:38—Both continue to flip through clip files and folders.

10:45—Other reporter leaves room.

10:46—A rattling in the air tubes from the courtroom to the press room can be heard. (This is the sign that the first opinion is on its way—the tube containing the slip of paper with the case number on it is being sent to the Press Officer who will then release decision to the newsmen in the press room.)

10:47—*Star* copy boy enters office with copy of majority opinion. It's case #291—an antitrust case in three parts. Bullen checks the vote. It's 5–2, with two justices not participating. Checks personal file. Finds one paragraph. Case appears to be relatively minor antitrust issue. Question: Should he try to handle case in a couple of paragraphs at end of his story, or should he let the business reporter handle it?

10:49—Calls national desk. Flips pages while resting phone receiver on his shoulder. Tells desk that first opinion out and that "it's a small business" thing. Holds off any decision until sees what else is coming that day.

10:50—Notes that first opinion was by [then] Justice Clark—thus only the senior-most justices are left for the day. (Justices announce opinions in order of seniority—those with the least number of years on the Court come first.) Continues to glance through the opinion.

10:53—Copy boy enters again. Press Officer says this is the "best thing" for the day. It's the Communist mail case, *Corliss Lamont* v. *Postmaster General.*

10:54—The Court has struck down the Post Office practice of withholding propaganda mail and destroying it unless requested by the addressee to be delivered. Vote is 8–0 in two parts. Bullen circles name of the majority opinion writer and writes in the vote on the first page. He starts to read the majority opinion, underlining quickly as he goes.

(10:55—First deadline passes.)

10:57—Copy boy comes in with the next case—#421—a Federal Communications Commission decision involving use of confidential documents. "It's not big." After glancing to see what it is, Bullen puts it on top of railing alongside his desk.

10:58—Continues to read the Communist mail case. Continues to mark passages of majority opinion.

11:00—Copy boy brings in another case. It's a right-to-legal-counsel issue in three parts. It's put aside immediately. Bullen picks up the phone and calls the national copy desk. He's ready to dictate. It's agreed that business story goes to business page reporter.

11:01—As dictationist at other end of phone gets ready, Bullen lays out the opinion and folders in front of him. He gives the story the identifying slugline "Mail" and starts to dictate: "The Post Office Department practice of holding up mail believed to be foreign Communist propaganda . . ." Double buzzer sounds indicating end of Court action for the day.

11:02—The copy boy brings in the order of the Court—the last items that will be handed down. Bullen continues: ". . . was struck down today by the Supreme Court as an infringement of . . .

11:03:—"First Amendment rights, period, paragraph. Justice William O. Douglas, who delivered the Court's (unanimous)[30] opinion, . . .

---

30. The exact word missed by the observer, but Bullen said afterwards he was quite sure he had said "unanimous." (This whole minute-by-minute diary was also checked later by Bullen—for accuracy of fact and interpretation.)

11:04—". . . said the decision was based on the fact that an addressee (a-d-d-r-e-s-s-e-e) was required to request that such detained mail be delivered . . . period, paragraph. 'This requirement is almost certain to have a deterrent effect,' Douglas said, 'especially as respects to those that have sensitive positions. . . .' "

11:05—Continues this procedure of filing story. Alternates between the opinion itself and paraphrasing of clippings and other notes.

11:24—Puts phone down briefly; pauses. Problem is minor one of wording—wants to leave situation a bit open because of possibility that change in Post Office procedure might bring different Court ruling later. Inserts phrase to this effect.

11:28—Tells dictationist at other end of phone to send copy along to national desk. Calls national desk to inform them insert is on the way.

11:30—Back to the dictationist and the story.

11:34—Looks at the concurring opinion by Justice Brennan for the first time.

11:35—Rests phone on shoulder. Reads opinion quickly.

11:37—Tells dictationist to mark another insert. Checks wall clock; 12:15 deadline is nearing. "Let me call you back. OK?" Cuts off line.

11:38—Dials national desk. Tells them another insert is coming.

11:40—Back to the dictationist. Makes a high insert based on concurring opinion.

11:42—Resumes quote from concurring opinion, attributing remarks to Justice Goldberg.

11:45—Corrects mistake; Justice Goldberg has concurred in the opinion, but it was written by Justice Brennan.[31]

11:46—Bullen expresses concern over the actual vote. Is opinion really unanimous? Decision is 8–0, but three justices are part of concurring opinion that has slightly different emphasis.

11:48—Resumes main part of story, emphasizing the fact that three justices concurred with slightly different view on the issue.

---

31. This mistake turned out to be a dilemma for the observer. The quick judgment was made at the time to step out of character as a researcher and to point out the discrepancy. In retrospect, the important observation seemed to be that the newsman's eye had caught the wrong name. How the error would be corrected—or even whether it would be—seemed secondary. To become such a participant was improper research procedure, but to hold back in this situation also might have upset the whole observation relationship.

11:51—Tells dictationist to send along what he has so far.

11:52—Wonders whether sent too much—but this seems to be the only thing that is "real newsy" so decided could go a little longer than usual.

11:53—Tells dictationist to hold on. Starts to scan other opinions left. Tells dictationist: "Mark 'folo'—The Court also had these other actions—"

11:54—Starts dictating civil rights story based on a brief, unsigned order. This follows the Communist mail story. After a lead paragraph, picks up four or five prepared paragraphs and reads from these. Shows first obvious signs of relaxing.

12:01—Starts dictating short story about Court agreeing to review libel case.

12:03—Scans other orders—pauses on Court refusal to hear a conviction of a home repairs firm. Checks notes and starts dictating short story.

12:11—Sets phone receiver down and looks at FCC opinion announced by Court.

12:13—Turns to notes on case.

12:15—Spots summary paragraph in opinion, picks up phone receiver, and quickly dictates paragraph. (Second deadline passes.)

12:16—Turns to opinion in right-to-counsel case. It was sent back with no Court action. Seems to involve habeas corpus questions.

12:17—Looks through concurring opinion in the case and starts to file another "folo" item. Stops, reads more of opinion.

12:24—Calls national desk to tell them he has a final news story that might be interesting. It may be a "sleeper"—including several views by the justices on procedural matters in criminal cases.

12:27—Reporter for second wire service (who has a separate office in main press room) enters Bullen's office. Bullen asks what reporter is doing on the right-to-counsel case. Reporter answers that he is going to read over it slowly—hasn't decided yet. Reporter asks about identification of person in civil rights case. Bullen says he isn't using full identification. Reporter leaves and heads toward press room; Bullen resumes study of right-to-counsel case.

12:30—Bullen asks wire service reporter across the room (with whom he shares office) whether reporter sees any "barnburners." Reply: Only the Communist mail case.[32]

12:33—Talks with national news desk. It's agreed to file separate story on criminal procedures matter. Wire service reporter leaves desk and goes out of room.

12:34—Bullen starts dictating story.

12:38—Shows sign again of relaxing.

12:42—Pauses, checks clock.[33] The 1:25 deadline nears but is still fairly far off.

12:47—Wire service reporter returns to desk—observes to wire service colleague that reporter (in press room) for competitive service is giving considerable attention to procedural matter story. Starts reading the opinion quickly.

12:48—Bullen finishes dictating. "That's all." Hangs up phone.

12:50—Starts checking through rest of orders.

12:51—Spots case not on previous order lists.

12:52—Checks case—finds it of primarily minor procedural interest. Decides not worth story.

12:53—Goes back to list. Calls national desk again.

12:54—Smiles, body relaxes.

12:55—"All have for you." Hangs up phone.

The Diary Interpreted

Everything but the criminal procedure story made the main 12:15 P.M. and 1:25 P.M. deadlines for the day. (The first five paragraphs of the Communist mail story also made a replate of the 10:55 A.M. edition.) In total, all of these May 24 stories ran about 1,100 words, or 34 column inches of type based on an eight-column format. (For the final version, see Appendix B.) The criminal procedure story, which ran about 450 words or another 13 column inches, appeared in all major editions of the *Star* on May 25. In addition, among other activities on the afternoon of the twenty-fourth, Bullen put together a follow-up story for the twenty-fifth that stressed congressional and Post Office Department reaction to the Communist mail case.

32. The wire service reporter and several of his colleagues had returned to the office ten to fifteen minutes earlier, but the exact time was not recorded.

33. Bullen probably partly did so because the observer had looked up at the wall clock. Bullen had just swung around so that the observer was suddenly in his line of vision.

Among the more significant comments on the sequence of events outlined in the diary, the following seem particularly important:

1) Decisions regarding a reporter's story selection and emphasis are hard to analyze precisely, but some patterns can be traced. During the period in the Court term studied, there were only fifteen or so cases left to be announced. Thus, Bullen had the advantage of knowing which cases were left, although he still had to prepare himself primarily by guessing. Clearly, he was not able to use much of his preparation time "efficiently."

By comparison with other cases that day, the Communist mail decision was stressed because it was probably the most important long-term legal issue and also the most "interesting" one. The decision was "newsworthy," in part, because the nature of the case provided controversy and conflict between big government and a citizen representing the view of a political minority.

Decisions in news selection at the Court depend most on what is available that day. With only a limited amount of time, Bullen must hastily establish a priority list. How much information he files on any one case depends largely on how much "weight" (space) he feels it deserves and how much detail he feels he needs to tell the story.

In tackling each Court opinion, Bullen finds himself constantly looking for clear statements by the justices of what has been decided. Sometimes he finds them quickly; other times he has to dig. He uses quotes from opinions partly to tell in the justices' words exactly what happened (what was said) and partly to provide color, emphasis, and change of pace in his story. He usually organizes each story in the traditional news writing pattern of trying to tell what is most important at the beginning. The vote of the Court is important; thus, he tries to get the voting breakdown near the top of the story.

2) The brief interaction among newsmen at the Court provides insight into how reporters keep an eye on what the competition is doing and supports those studies that have stressed the possible importance of newsmen's peer groups.[34] In this particular situation, it seemed clear that Bullen's passing reference to another reporter about the

34. See especially: Cohen, *The Press and Foreign Policy*, and Warren Breed, "Social Control in the Newsroom," in Wilbur Schramm (ed.), *Mass Communications* (Urbana: University of Illinois Press, 1960), pp. 178–94.

criminal procedures case helped set up a "chain reaction" of extra attention to this decision. Although neither wire service went into much detail on the case, it is significant to note the circularity in the evolution of a news story. One newsman can become especially interested in a story after becoming aware of another reporter's interest.

The newsmen's interaction illustrates the notion that the reporter is often "haunted by the professional necessity to validate his news sense." [35] Not only does it help to know what others are doing for competitive reasons, but it also can help, after the fact, to have news judgments reinforced.

3) Bullen acknowledges that his philosophy in news judgment tends to be conservative. He tries to guard against minor loopholes in Court opinions that might limit the decisions. He prefers to be on the safe side—understating rather than overstating what the Court has decided. He tends to limit his interpretation to the specific case at hand and to avoid any sweeping statements that might carry the case much beyond the issues involved.

Perhaps the best example of this caution was Bullen's preference for the expression "8–0 decision" over "8–0 opinion" in the Communist mail case. He was worried that the opinion technically was 5–3 and not 8–0. In the final news story, however, the copy desk left the wording as "8–0 opinion." Another example is that Bullen prefers to use the word "indicated" instead of "said" in situations where there is no explicit reference to a statement in the opinion. "Indicated" is used by him more for interpretative situations; "said" is used where the reference is more directly stated.

Part of such conservative approaches can be traced to Bullen's training in law. He is extremely sensitive to shades of legal meaning and how a certain word might make the copy "technically wrong." But part of this sensitivity seems to be a matter of temperament and a certain necessary uncertainty in the often complex and fast-moving news situation.

On this same conservative theme, it is significant to note Bullen's frequent interaction (seven separate calls) with his national news desk.

35. Cohen, *The Press and Foreign Policy*, p. 81.

Some newsmen feel there is a danger in overdoing such contact—just as some see problems in being overcautious in news judgments. But Bullen's view, again, is that it is usually safer to communicate than not to. (Such interaction with news desks is common among other Court newsmen but obviously is not necessarily a typical practice in most news work. In fact, many times reporters and editors will work very independently with little or no discussion of the story written or planned.)

A variety of positive, negative, and neutral implications could be read into parts of this case study. But rather than focus here on such possible value judgments, this moment-by-moment approach has simply sought to stress some of the most significant patterns in news decision-making by one Court reporter.

Distribution of Activity

The preceding sequence can also be illustrated schematically to get an overview of the patterns of the flow of news information in and out:

Fig. 1.—A DECISION DAY AT THE COURT (MAY 24, 1965)

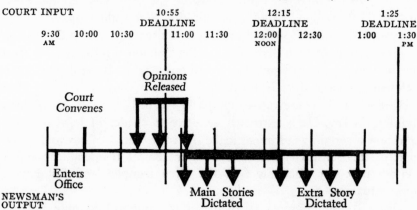

Washington Star newsman faced three deadlines—10:55 A.M., 12:15 and 1:25 P.M. Court's opinions were released within fifteen minutes—10:46 to 11:01. Dictation of first story started at 11:00 and lasted until 11:51, with remaining stories squeezed in before main 12:15 deadline. Special story and other items were handled from 12:15 to 12:55; reporter, thus, finished thirty minutes before final deadline.

DIFFERENCES IN THE APPROACH TO NEWS

Questions of News Philosophy

At first glance it would seem that a "news story is a news story"—that journalists might vary in the news item produced but would approach a story on a given Supreme Court decision in much the same manner. Such is not the case, however.

Much of the variation in Court stories depends on variations in *how much* the Court is covered and *when* it has to be covered. For example, the "regulars" such as the *New York Times, Washington Post, Washington Evening Star,* Associated Press, and United Press International all attempt to cover the Court "thoroughly" each term. There are perhaps another dozen or so news organizations which might be considered in the "regular" or "near regular" categories. The important dimension distinguishing these groups, however, tends to be deadlines. At the high-speed end of the continuum would be the wire services, which work on the philosophy of getting out the story as quickly as possible. The AP and UPI are interested most in the "what happened." At the other end of the continuum, although also under some deadline pressures, are such newspapers as the *New York Times* and *Washington Post.* As morning papers, their reporters usually have most of a decision day to get their copy into shape. In between these extremes of the continuum fall papers such as the *Washington Evening Star* which, as noted in the previous section, attempts to get both speed and depth into its regular Court coverage.

Besides the regular or semiregular news media organizations, there are a variety of others around the Court on any one decision day, representing such diverse groups as Religious News Service, the Associated Negro Press, Bender's Tax Service, the Association of American Railroads, and the National Association of Manufacturers. Various legal publications such as *U.S. Law Week* and those of Commerce Clearing House are among those most interested in the opinions. But the extent of their news reporting is limited. As "legal services," they distribute full opinions primarily and are not usually interested in the traditional media approaches of news highlights and summaries.

Of all the mass news media covering the Court, however, the wire services are probably the most significant because of the sheer numbers of readers served. Even though both the *New York Times* and *Los Angeles Times-Washington Post* news syndicates have increased their scope in recent years, the AP and UPI still are providing the bulk of information on the Court. Most of the 1750 or so daily papers throughout the country are getting much of their Washington news from the wire services. Even those larger papers with Washington bureaus rely heavily on the wire services for Court coverage unless there is a case of special interest to be covered. Most of the radio and television coverage comes first from either the AP and UPI newspaper or radio-television news tickers. And, although such publications as *Time, Newsweek,* and *U.S. News and World Report* often have part-time reporters at the Court, the wire services are also used widely for weekly news roundups. And perhaps most importantly, it is the AP and UPI news files that provide much of the background for editorial writers, columnists, and commentators for news organizations of all sizes. Thus, the news philosophies of the Associated Press and United Press International with regard to Court coverage are worth special attention here.

Although AP and UPI newsmen have time to pore over the briefs, to prepare background notes on cases, and to write up parts of stories in advance, once the news breaks there is an overriding emphasis on speed. Often there is special stress on the reaction of public and private "name figures" to the decision.

The wire services are intensely competitive because their purpose is to serve clients or members.[36] (The AP is basically an association of member papers and stations, while UPI is a private organization with clients.) The organizations are very similar in their approaches to news gathering and editing. There is a premium on fast news. There are edition deadlines and news broadcasts to meet; without "fresh" and "important" news there is not much of a product for the wire services to sell.

In this economic situation, it is not surprising that the AP and UPI should be intensely preoccupied with "beating" each other. In a sense, each wire service is always eager to get a story that the other does

36. Much of the data in this section is based on an interview with Charlotte Moulton, UPI reporter at the Court, May 7, 1965, and with other wire service personnel, including four news executives or news managers for AP and UPI in Washington and New York City, May–June, 1965.

not have. But because today exclusive stories are not frequent, each is anxious to get there sooner and more often—either to those news organizations that carry both services or to those that use only one service but might be in the market to switch. Thus, many times the standard is simply: how many papers (and which papers) carried your story? Did you beat the competition?

A common theme during interviews with wire service personnel was the view that AP and UPI allow a *New York Times* or *Washington Post*, or a Walter Lippmann or James Reston, to do what they do. The wire services, it is argued, are meant to serve everybody and by so doing protect those papers and individuals that want to devote themselves to special news topics or to interpretative analyses. To a large extent the wire services do enable other news media to provide more thorough coverage. At the same time, however, many papers and radio and TV stations throughout the country are not really using the wire services as "backstops"; the AP and UPI often become the primary or exclusive source of Washington and other nation-wide coverage.

In the specific setting at the Court—as in other news fields—the wire services face multiple problems. Their news tickers can carry only so many words per minute (slightly more than a word a second is an average figure). This means that the various national, regional, state, and special news wires are restricted in how much news they can carry in a certain space of time. There is an upper limit on what can be carried—"a capacity to the channel." [37]

This means that the wire services are forced constantly to weigh potential reader-listener interest in news stories. Decisions have to be made concerning whether a news item on fighting in Vietnam should be carried before a Supreme Court decision on civil rights. And how much should be carried on each story? Should part of the text of the Court opinion be sent out? Can such use of time and space be justified in light of other news that day?

There are also the never-ending problems of staffing. The AP and UPI Washington bureaus may have two or three reporters available to cover the Court on decision days but additional personnel usually

37. Cf. especially: Wilbur Schramm, "Information Theory and Mass Communication," *Journalism Quarterly*, 32(1955):140.

will be in short supply. Reporters simply are needed elsewhere—perhaps to cover a major bill debate in Congress; a visit to Washington by two of the latest astronauts; the latest picket march near the White House; an afternoon press conference by the Secretary of Defense; or three or four speeches by visiting dignitaries. In addition, there are all the other regular governmental news beats that need to be checked. There are the possible Washington angles stemming from the latest crisis in South America, plus the half-dozen or so requests for special regional-interest stories from news clients.

Even though in recent years more wire service personnel have been freed to do interpretative and analytical pieces, the bulk of the news coverage continues to be heavily "spot news"—partly because of the basic struggle just to cover the events of any one day.

One crucial result of such pressure is the constant need to make quick decisions. Wire service Court coverage often becomes so fast-moving that there is no time to sit back and see where the story or stories are going.

To try to meet the problems of pressure in Court news coverage, the wire services have stressed preparedness. Many stories are written in advance with alternate leads prepared; sometimes these will be mailed out to regional bureaus. The moment the decision is announced, the wire service reporters at the Court spring into action and release the prepared copy. These early stories often carry only the barest outline of what happened with perhaps a paragraph or two of background material.[38]

After this outline of the decision has been sent out on the news wires, the Court newsmen often will rewrite the lead of the story and insert more detailed information on the Court's thinking. There is usually heavy emphasis on a few paragraphs of quoted material from the majority and minority opinions. Sometimes, if the advance copy is considered unsuitable, an entirely new story will be filed. In any case, the basic philosophy is to rush out the "what happened," then later to add some of the details.

---

38. Despite such haste it is significant that no examples of mixed-up alternative leads in recent years, at least, have been found. Wire service personnel are especially aware of this danger of picking the wrong lead and have been able to avoid such errors by carefully matching case numbers and decisions and by double-checking results.

The prepared-copy approach has become very much a fact of life for the Court wire service reporters; it is seen as the most efficient means of getting decisions out quickly. A major decision of the Court, for example, can be on news tickers across the country within five minutes of release in the courtroom. This speed enables many papers with 11:30 A.M., noon, or 1:00 P.M. deadlines to get at least part of the Court's activity into early afternoon editions. Radio and television stations are able to carry spot items on noon broadcasts.

This preparedness also helps in handling the flood of Court orders. Denials and grants of certiorari can be covered in mass numbers by setting up such alternative lead paragraphs as "agreed to hear" or "refused to intervene." Since most Court orders give no explanation or commentary by the justices, this approach allows the story in a sense to be covered "fully" the moment the outcome is known. It is usually left to local news organizations to get any local comment on the Court action.

Perhaps the most revealing example of this wire service news philosophy is the method used to report a lengthy Court decision. If the whole opinion cannot be stuffed in the container by an assistant in the courtroom and sent to the reporters in the booths below, then often the last page will be torn off first. The last line, with the all-important word "reverse" or "affirm," helps to launch the story faster.

Despite such emphasis on preparedness and speed, wire service reporters at the Court spend significant amounts of time in more leisurely preparation of news stories. Usually after the initial flurry of decisions, there are "roundup" stories to be assembled in which most of the Court action is summarized into one news item. Or there are follow-up stories to write, with perhaps new emphases and detail on the Court action for the next morning's papers. Often such efforts are handled by desk men in the Washington bureaus; they are essentially "rewrites"—which just rephrase and repackage the original efforts by reporters at the Court, possibly adding information about public reaction or other related happenings.

Most typical of this more leisurely end of the continuum are the *New York Times* and *Washington Post*. Although there are many papers (such as the *Washington Evening Star*) that fall somewhere between these and the wire services on the speed dimension, a brief analysis here of the *Times* and *Post* provides an especially meaningful contrast with the wire service approaches toward news.

Not unrelated to the speed factor is the fact that the *Times* and *Post* are usually ranked high in prestige around the Court, not only by justices and Court staff but also by other newsmen. (These newspapers, of course, enjoy similar prestige in other fields such as politics and foreign affairs.) The two papers are "information leaders" among the press corps; although newsmen do not always agree with their editorial policy and minimize talk about how good they are, there is no question that most journalists consider them worthwhile to read.[39]

The philosophy behind the *Times* is, in overview, that each person who reads a paper usually has special interests. These may be the arts, baseball, British association football scores, the arrival of buyers, politics, or the law. The *Times* has simply applied this concept to the Supreme Court. The result is coverage that attempts to meet the needs of the person with unusual degrees of interest and background in the law.[40] Obviously, too, the paper is also aiming its coverage at the public official or private citizen who wants or needs to know what the Court is doing.

The *Post*'s situation, while often reaching many of the same types of public leaders and educated citizens, is somewhat different. The *Post*, more than the *Times*, attempts to be a paper of both international and local scope, and it tends to focus on a narrower audience—specifically providing news commentary and opinion for reasonably intelligent and interested government workers, officials, and citizens in the Washington area.

Procedural differences for *Times* and *Post* newsmen vary with the individuals assigned to the Court; but, in general, reporters for both papers tend to follow closely the oral arguments and oral announce-

39. See especially: Cohen, *The Press and Foreign Policy*; Rivers, *The Opinionmakers*; Leo Rosten, *The Washington Correspondents* (New York: Harcourt, Brace and Co., 1937), and Warren Breed, "Newspaper 'Opinion Leaders' and the Processes of Standardization," *Journalism Quarterly*, 32(1955): 280.

40. Based mainly on an interview with Reston, May 26, 1965. Reston himself has also been credited with saying that he writes for the lonely professor at some college in a small town in the Midwest who cares and who wants some of the complicated issues of the day clarified by a friend. Noted in David Halberstam, "Love, Life, and Selling Out in Poland," *Harper's*, July, 1967, p. 80.

ments of opinions. Both also tend more than other Court newsmen to have extensive personal contacts with lawyers throughout Washington, especially those in the Solicitor General's office who are labeled (as close followers of the Court) as the "Supreme Court Bar."

Even for *Times* or *Post* newsmen, with the great advantage of late-afternoon deadlines for news copy, there is still the obvious pressure of time. Anything that can save time in one place can help free it elsewhere—perhaps allowing for lunch with attorneys from the Solicitor General's office who might provide helpful background for understanding and perspective on a case.

In this analysis of varied approaches, however, an even more meaningful contrast in covering the Court can be found than between the AP or UPI and *Times* or *Post*. It is the often dramatic difference between the Court "regulars" and the "irregulars." The less regular group includes most of the newsmen who cover the Court on decision days.[41] They vary greatly in their methods.

Some try to drop by every day or two to research major cases that might be coming up. Often these reporters, although perhaps responsible for several other Washington beats, arrive on decision days fairly well prepared. (One advantage they have is that they usually don't have to cover all or even most cases announced. Attention typically is centered only on those of major importance or regional interest.) Others in this occasional group may just wander into the building on decision days or may use a combination of telephone and wire service stories to put together a by-lined article.

It is not a subjective judgment to conclude that many reporters appear at the Court without knowing very much about what is going on. A newsman may breeze in from out of town to cover the second day of an oral argument; he may spend much of his first few moments in the courtroom trying to figure out exactly which justice is which.[42]

41. This group includes some from radio and television and magazines, but the bulk of news reporters present are from newspapers, wire services, and news syndicates.

42. Along with a press pass card, the Press Officer distributes a small slip of paper with a diagram of the bench in the courtroom and an identification of where each justice (based on seniority) sits.

Such a style has been sometimes labeled, perhaps quite appropriately, as the "spasmodic approach."

And, of course, there are the many columnists and editorial writers who include the Court in their other writing efforts on government and society. Some, such as James Marlow of the Associated Press, have acquired a reputation among newsmen and legal experts for being well-read and especially knowledgeable on the Court. Like most columnists and editorial writers, Marlow can do much of his research and writing a day or so after a decision has been handed down. He can compile an extensive file of clippings and wire copy which, when combined with copies of the actual opinions, can provide a fairly large resource of information for an analytical or "opinion" piece.[43]

The point is that, in theory, the Supreme Court can be covered analytically even though the writer may not be on the scene most of the time. In practice, news magazines, for example, often cover it this way.[44] But equally important is the fact that for many of the Court newsmen, the job becomes very much part-time—the Court is just one news beat among several or many. In contrast with the regular full-time Court newsmen, such part-timers usually cover just the "big cases" and those of "special interest."

What Is "News"?

In 1947, the Commission on Freedom of the Press (the Robert Hutchins Commission) concluded:

> The word "news" has come to mean something quite different from important news information. When a journalist says that a certain event is news, he does not mean that it is important in itself. Often it is; but about as often it is not. The journalist means by news something that has happened within the last few hours which will attract the interest of the customers. The criteria of interest are recency or firstness, proximity, combat, human interest, and novelty. Such criteria limit accuracy and significance.[45]

43. Details on method from interview with Marlow, June 1, 1965.
44. *Time* magazine has been especially successful with this approach (combined with on-the-scene coverage by members of its Washington staff) since starting its section on "The Law," Oct. 18, 1963.
45. *A Free and Responsible Press* (Chicago: University of Chicago Press, 1947), pp. 54–55.

The press has never quite forgiven the Hutchins Commission for its attacks and proposals. But rather than debate the merits of this argument, the important analytical point here is that this particular statement is still for the most part true more than twenty years later. Media standards for defining what is or is not news have not changed greatly; nor have they become much more precise.

"Reporters have great difficulty in putting into words just what they are hunting for each day"; there are "no precise definitions and understandings of what constitutes news. . . ." [46]

As with the judge who may have a hard time explaining his work, this inability to put into words what one does is not necessarily bad. In fact, one value of any intellectual process may be the lack of restraint imposed by inflexible definitions. Some editors, for example, acknowledge the great difficulty in describing what they do and how they do it but, in the end, do not seem overly concerned or affected by the problem.[47] There seems to be a certain—often healthy—intuition in news work that cannot be spelled out clearly either for those in the business or for those not in it.

But questions about what news is are still important because reporters and editors are definers of news by their selection process. And the question becomes even more important with problems of circularity: news is what gets in the newspaper or is broadcast. "What was reported is news; what was not reported—for whatever reasons—is not news." [48]

Press coverage of the Supreme Court includes both traditional and special definitions of news. But the evidence collected is that, indeed, criteria of judgment tend to be vague and flexible rather than specific and firm. One obvious end result is the wide range in standards for news selection and emphasis among the many media organizations covering the Court.

Traditional elements such as "important events," "big names," or "unusual cases" all are part of the Court newsman's general standards. While these concepts often cannot be pinned down specifically, it can be argued they do have considerable common-sense logic about them.

46. Cohen, *The Press and Foreign Policy*, p. 54.
47. See, for example: John Fischer, "The Editor's Trade," *Harper's*, July, 1965, pp. 16-24.
48. Cohen, *The Press and Foreign Policy*, p. 59.

Another traditional view of news is that it is, more simply, "factual information." Hidden in this concept is perhaps the most essential criterion for all newswork: accuracy. Factual information is "accurate" information; accuracy is both a part of the definition of news and an objective of the newsman. Thus, even with the wire services working at the Court, speed is far below accuracy in priority. This conclusion is based on more than just verbal expression by Court newsmen of what they do; it can be easily observed as a part of the press institution. Definition of the term and extent of dedication to it will vary among newsmen, but all realize they could hurt their cause or lose their jobs if they became consistently "inaccurate" gatherers of news. (The variation, "gatherers of 'inaccurate' news," is quite a different concept and is discussed later in analysis and evaluation of press performance.)

Just as accuracy is both a definition of news and a goal of the newsman, so are such concepts as interest, usefulness, speed, and completeness. News is often something that is interesting, useful, recent, and "fully reported." A newsman may decide to use a certain word because it is "more interesting." Or, he will rush out a bulletin on a Court case because he feels people will want to know about the event "quickly."

Conflict and controversy are also universal standards in news work—often reflected in the concepts of interest and importance. But conflicts and controversies before the Court are different than in most news situations. Instead of the more emotional political issues, there is supposed to be (and usually is) a more reserved combat among legal issues. The Court newsman has to work within the framework of these issues. He is given less room for interpretation than reporters covering politics around the Capitol or the White House.

The legal issues involved may not be very interesting for the layman, but the newsman knows that once he strays too far into popularizing he will no longer be covering a court of law. This restriction imposed on legal news at the Court may go a long way in explaining why Court newsmen often show considerable deference to the institution. They must go along with the Court because the Court is the definer of the legal issues—and, thus, the interpreter of much of the news. Perhaps the Court's standards of news judgment are imposed upon newsmen to a greater extent than those in any other field of governmental activity. Certainly, by comparison, the Capitol Hill reporter has much greater freedom to determine what to write about and how to get at it.

Throughout the process of selecting and defining news and choosing the words with which to convey it, reporters and editors are hounded by the problem of their audiences. There is the constant tug between a desire to use as few words as possible (so that more information can be squeezed in) and a concern to use enough words so that the reader or listener will know what is going on.

In a sense, then, news is what can be communicated to audiences. Partly by definition, it is something that has happened that is capable of being understood. Sometimes a reporter or editor will make a news judgment explicitly on this basis: "Oh, the readers wouldn't understand that," or "This needs to be put in simpler language."

One former Court newsman who was interviewed explained part of the problem thus:

> A story should be understandable to the lay reader but should not be incorrect. The problem is that some reporters so oversimplify what the Court has done as to make them wrong in the minds of lawyers. I think the art is to oversimplify when it is necessary but to add a phrase which lets your more sophisticated readers know that you know what you are doing.

This delicate balance, indeed, is one of the primary problems facing the Court newsman, especially one who includes the justices among his "sophisticated readers." One of the audiences for the newsman may well be his news sources. Although the degree of concern with what the justices might think varies among newsmen at the Court, there is little doubt that much of the audience pressure comes from within the Court Building.

Perhaps the single best example of the audience-anticipation problem lies in the term "certiorari." Even reporters for the *New York Times, Washington Post,* or *Wall Street Journal* noted in interviews that they usually try to avoid using the term in news stories. More general expressions are sought—such as "brought before" or "agreed to review." Many times even the sophisticated reader does not really know what certiorari means. And even more likely, he does not really care. The Court reporter then is faced with a relatively minor, but very representative, type of news dilemma. He must either stop his story and define the term or he must seek a simpler way of saying the same thing. With "certiorari," a word relevant to many Court news stories, the simpler phrasing tends to be found by newsmen as the more satisfactory of two not very satisfactory approaches. Thus, the complex act of the Court denying a writ of certiorari becomes transformed into something like: "The Supreme Court today declined to hear the case of. . . ." The simpler idea becomes "the news happening."

The News Story Transmitted

On the above pages, attention has been focused on the newsman at the Court. This is appropriate because obviously what gets in the paper depends heavily on what comes from the reporter on the scene. But after the news story is filed by the Court reporter, several important sequences take place that need brief analysis—especially before the case examinations of news coverage which will be presented in the next chapter.

With the "need" for editors to add reactions to Court decisions and to weigh the Court news against other stories, there is a constant expanding and contracting process. In general, the amount of news originally sent is trimmed and its content "polished." Sometimes the stories are drastically reduced or eliminated completely by a newspaper or wire service's Washington bureau. For the wire services especially, there is also the further gatekeeping process at regional bureaus. Often the flow of wire copy looks like a funnel where the amount that reaches the newspaper reader has gone through a series of reductions—from perhaps 500 words by the Court newsman, to 350 sent out by the Washington editors, to 300 sent out by regional editors, to 150 selected for final use by the national wire news editor on the paper.[49]

Early versions of Court stories tend not to be edited to any great extent and are sent out much as originally written by Court re-

---

49. If a story is of special local significance, however, often the flow of news will look less like an inverted pyramid and more like an hourglass—starting with a subtracting process and then a building up again near the end.

porters. Most of any changes come at later stages through local editing and headline writing or when deskmen in Washington rewrite stories for next-day consumption. This situation tends to hold true for both newspaper and wire service copy.

One reason is, indeed, that reporters at the Court are generally considered to be more knowledgeable on their subjects than other newsmen. In such cases where specialties are involved, both veteran and inexperienced deskmen and editors tend to leave a reporter's copy alone. Minor changes will be made, but deskmen simply are hesitant to make drastic changes in wording or emphasis. If any drastic revision is made it will tend to be done most often simply by cutting off the story near the end. A 15-column-inch article on the Court is treated much like most news stories—in both the original writing and later editing. Less important material is usually placed near the end; the more important highlights come first. Although this "inverted pyramid" style of writing has serious drawbacks, it does make sense, as it is often the quickest and safest way to work with a piece of copy that is too long to be fitted into the space or time allotted.

Throughout the country, then, newspaper readers or broadcast listeners are getting only a small percentage of the news sent out on any one day. Even the *New York Times*—with supposedly "all the news that's fit to print"—is able to print only about 15 per cent of the million or so words that flow in each day.[50]

There are, therefore, significant forces at work on the news of the Court apart from the newsman's daily struggles at the Court Building. Many of these can be related—in sweeping terms—to the obvious economic and bureaucratic elements in the news institutions.

For example, one can note the necessary influence of management in such vastly varying decisions as: How many newsmen can and should be assigned to the Court? What kind of news coverage should be provided? Indeed, economic and philosophical concerns go a long way in determining what a reporter at the Court will send out in the first place. Many of these choices are in the hands of the reporters; but obviously results depend greatly on what the reporter is told to do by his superiors and what, in effect, he is allowed to do. He is also influenced by his peers, and social and psychological forces

50. As estimated, among others, by Cohen, *The Press and Foreign Policy*, p. 113.

are at work, stemming from both his specific news organization and the mores of his profession.

> The newsman's source of rewards is located not among readers, who are manifestly his clients, but among his colleagues and superiors. Instead of adhering to societal and professional ideals, he redefines his values to the more pragmatic level of the newsroom group.[51]

The newsman is, in part, writing to please someone to whom he is responsible. He likely has had to undergo some adjustment in his own thinking as he learns to work with others who will be working with his copy. The experienced newsman, as he gains self-confidence in a news organization, will tend to think much less in terms of what someone else wants. But often, in fact, he is not writing any less for someone else; he is just thinking less about this as a problem. He may not be fully conscious of the pressures on him, or he may simply learn not to care as much about them. He may develop more independence and may show considerable initiative, yet in his early experience he has undergone a significant period of assimilation.

Thus, added to the already complicated task of communicating to both lay and sophisticated audiences in the law (including the justices) is the intricate machinery of the whole news transmission process—complete with all its habits, traditions, pressures, economic considerations, and institutional, managerial, and individual philosophies or idiosyncrasies. The newsmen at the Court work in news environments of greatly varying standards. These environmental factors are crucial in any assessment of press performance at the Court.

51. Breed, "Social Control in the Newsroom," in Schramm, *Mass Communications*, p. 194.

IV

Case Studies
of News Coverage

THE PRAYER DECISIONS COMPARED

THERE IS AT FIRST GLANCE only limited value in analyzing the 1962 New York Regents prayer case (*Engel* v. *Vitale*); press treatment of that case has already been widely discussed.[1] But differences in interpretation do exist that need stressing, and several especially meaningful patterns evolve when the 1962 case is contrasted with the 1963 Bible reading and Lord's Prayer decision (*School District of Abington Township* v. *Schempp*).

The 1962 case caused a furor; the 1963 case stirred relatively little reaction. Why did the 1962 decision create probably the greatest publicity explosion ever to greet a decision about religion? Why, compared with 1962, did the nation receive the Court's 1963 decision with calm? The Court received more than 5,000 letters in 1962 but probably less than 100 in 1963. All this occurred even though the 1963 decision was of broader significance.[2]

1. Especially by William A. Hachten, "Jounalism and the Prayer Decision," *Columbia Journalism Review*, Fall, 1962, pp. 4–9; Winter, 1963, p. 54; and Chester A. Newland, "Press Coverage of the United States Supreme Court," *Western Political Quarterly*, 17(1964): 15–36.
2. See Paul Blanshard, *Religion and the Schools* (Boston: Beacon Press, 1963), *passim*; and Alpheus T. Mason and William M. Beaney, *American Constitutional Law* (Englewood Cliffs, N.J.: Prentice-Hall, 1964), p. 557; also from interview with Justice Tom C. Clark, June 10, 1965.

The following critical analysis of the two cases attempts to answer these questions and to pull out some of the elements of press coverage that have most lasting analytical significance.

Preparedness

An essential difference between *Engel* in 1962 and *Schempp* in 1963 was simply that more people were "ready" for the second case— not only many of the interested publics, but also the press and apparently the justices themselves. The first decision, although it certainly could have been anticipated by observers of the Court, was simply a shock for many. So, too, apparently was the public uproar for members of the Court.

By contrast, before the 1963 decision, church groups had comments ready—many of them favorable—in anticipation of the Court's announcement.[3] The year's period of "meditation" between the decisions had allowed many public figures, religious leaders, and others to learn more about what the Court had decided in overturning a state-sponsored school prayer. It also was easy to look ahead and expect that the Court would act the same way in "outlawing" Bible reading and the Lord's Prayer as incompatible with the concept of freedom of religion or establishment of religion (separation of church and state) expressed in the First Amendment.

The very issues involved in the *Engel* case were bound to be emotional and confusing. Religion is salient in the lives of many—especially when the usual Christian majorities suddenly find they are put in the position of having to give way to minority religious groups or "even atheists." And, at first appearance, the *Engel* decision seemed to be self-contradictory and did not make much sense. How could the Court ban prayers in schools and yet really be in favor of religion?

Here would seem to be a situation where lack of public understanding of the establishment clause of the First Amendment was a sub-

3. See James E. Clayton, *The Making of Justice* (New York: E. P. Dutton & Co., 1964), p. 275. The *New York Times* carried a page 1 story on the morning of June 17: "High Court Ruling On School Prayer Is Expected Today." Such an advance story was possible because the Court had designated the seventeenth in advance as the final day of the term.

stantial factor in the confusion.[4] Without some understanding of the subtlety and history of the clause, both public official and average citizen were at an immediate disadvantage in trying to figure out what the Court was saying.

Compounding this initial confusion were at least two other factors which even informed critics or supporters of the Court had to wrestle with.

Justice Douglas' concurring opinion in *Engel* indicated the first difficulty of precedent and inconsistency:

> My problem today would be uncomplicated but for *Everson* v. *Board of Education* 330 U.S. 1, 17, which allowed taxpayers' money to be used to pay "the bus fares of parochial school pupils as a part of a general program under which" the fares of pupils attending public and other schools were also paid. The *Everson* case seems in retrospect to be out of line with the First Amendment. . . .[5]

The second problem involved the other existing religious practices. It was perhaps best illustrated by this description in a political cartoon that appeared shortly after the decision. A small boy and his mother are sitting in the courtroom. The Court Crier is saying: "God Save the United States and this Honorable Court." The boy points toward the Crier and with a bewildered expression on his face turns toward his mother: "But Mommy isn't that unconstitutional?"[6]

The wording of majority and minority opinions did not fully anticipate these questions by answering them completely or clearly enough. There is, in fact, considerable evidence that the justices also did not fully understand each other.[7]

Although Justice Douglas was careful to point out that the *Engel* decision was an "extremely narrow one," this comment apparently got buried in the avalanche of doubts he raised elsewhere. "It was Justice Douglas, not news reporters and Court critics, who first raised the

4. Leonard Levy, "School Prayers and the Founding Fathers," *Commentary*, 34(1962): 225.
5. 370 U.S. 437, 443.
6. By Canfield of the *Newark News*. The original drawing can be found among many other cartoons on a wall in the Court press room.
7. Conclusion reinforced especially by Newland, "Press Coverage of the United States Supreme Court," p. 25.

point that numerous common ceremonial observances of a religious type might be banned by the logic of this decision." [8]

By listing in a footnote such aids to religion as tax-exempt status, Justice Douglas raised many questions. But critics of his opinion point out that he did not seem to answer them. Indeed, the various opinions of the justices seemed to be more of an internal struggle than a firm declaration of the legal issues involved.

Probably most representative of this struggle was Justice Black's footnote 21, which has become one of the most criticized "asides" in Court history. In retrospect, the footnote did seem to be extremely important to the majority opinion—so much so "it should never have been relegated to the bottom of the page." [9] Justice Black wrote:

> There is of course nothing in the decision reached here that is inconsistent with its fact that school children and others are officially encouraged to express love for our country by reciting historical documents such as the Declaration of Independence which contain references to the Deity or by singing officially espoused anthems which include the composer's profession of faith in a Supreme Being, or with the fact that there are many manifestations in our public life of belief in God. Such patriotic or ceremonial occasions bear no true resemblance to the unquestioned religious exercise that the State of New York has sponsored in this instance.

But an important consideration must be added here that helps explain this footnote. The evidence, although sketchy and not directly obtainable from sources interviewed, indicates the following:

Footnote 21 was not just casually tossed in to be hidden away in the majority opinion. It was largely the product of the Court's internal decision-making process and apparently the direct result of compromise. The exact sequence and details are uncertain, but the footnote apparently was written near the end of the opinion-writing stage. There was difficulty in getting agreement on wording and where the words should be located. Apparently the footnote was used because certain justices resisted including the material in the body of the majority opinion. Also, it seemingly was added with the "best of intentions" as an effort to give emphasis and clarity.

8. *Ibid.*
9. Blanshard, *Religion and the Schools*, p. 47. This view also was expressed by several newsmen and close observers of the Court who were interviewed.

The irony, of course, is that instead of helping much, the footnote was largely overlooked during early readings of the case. And, once discovered, it ended up adding considerable doubt. Why was this seemingly important statement in a footnote? Maybe it was not important after all? And how could this footnote be squared against Justice Douglas' footnote?

Whatever all the reasons for such confusion in the *Engel* case, it is clear that by 1963—besides various publics and the press being more prepared—the Court had also learned its lesson. Since the justices apparently were shaken by the 1962 protests, they took considerable care in the *Schempp* case to avoid a recurrence of the confusion. Specific steps taken included: (1) assignment of Justice Clark, with his simple and direct writing style and public relations sensitivity, to write the majority opinion; (2) emphasis in the majority opinion on the importance of religion and on historical background for perspective; (3) a seventy-seven-page concurring opinion by Justice Brennan and a shorter concurring opinion by Justice Goldberg that stressed the scope of the decision—what had been decided and what had not been decided.[10]

Throughout the opinion-writing process in *Schempp*, the justices had the distinct advantage of being able to fall back on their *Engel* decision. Not only did they have a precedent with which to work, they also had the advantage of a full year of public exposure to the principles involved. The Court took advantage of this extra time and background. Although it is hard to isolate causes and effects, the extra effort did seem to pay off as one reason for more acceptance and understanding of the 1963 decision.

What Happened in the Press

In comparing *Engel* and *Schempp* press coverage, it is important to start with a minor but significant time difference. Both opinions were handed down as part of busy final decision days, but the 1963 case came about twenty minutes earlier in the day. Justice Black

10. From, in sequence: (1) John P. Frank, *The Warren Court* (New York: Macmillan Company, 1964), p. 79, and Clayton, *The Making of Justice*, p. 284; (2) interview with Justice Clark, June 10, 1965, and (3) an address by Judge Irving R. Kaufman, Tulane Law Review Association, New Orleans, April 29, 1965.

started reading *Engel* at about 11:50 A.M. on June 25, 1962; Justice Clark started reading *Schempp* at about 11:30 A.M. on June 17, 1963. This extra few minutes gave wire services and local papers more time to work with the later case—at that crucial time of day when many news media are facing demanding deadlines.

The following analysis focuses on AP and UPI coverage—partly because of their nationwide scope in covering these decisions but primarily because the wire service coverage of *Engel* is where most criticism and attention has been placed.[11]

In both *Engel* and *Schempp*, the AP and UPI were out with bulletins within five minutes of the start of announcing the cases in the courtroom. The lead paragraphs in *Engel* were especially important:

11:54 A.M. Bulletin:
Washington, June 25 (AP)—The Supreme Court ruled today the offering of a 22–word daily prayer in New York State's public schools violates the U.S. Constitution.

12:02 P.M.—First Add:
Five parents with children in schools in New Hyde Park, N.Y., had questioned the practice as a violation of the principle of separation of church and state. . . .

11:58 A.M. Bulletin:
Washington, June 25 (UPI)—The Supreme Court ruled today that daily recital of an official state prayer in public schools, even though non-compulsory, offends the religious freedom guarantees in the Constitution.

11:58 A.M.—First Add:
The 6–1 decision came in a New York case but will affect many thousands of schools throughout the country. . . .

In the above news leads, the most significant point is that the AP story failed to stress the idea of a state-supported prayer but had been careful to note the concept of separation of church and state,

---

11. Case material throughout this section comes from a variety of sources, including: Hachten, "Journalism and the Prayer Decision"; Newland, "Press Coverage of the United States Supreme Court"; and Clayton, *The Making of Justice*—plus, where available, original documents and newspapers on microfilm. In particular, Hachten made available some of his research source materials in a letter dated June 16, 1965.

while the UPI story stressed the official state prayer aspect but used the vague term "religious freedom guarantees." Thus, critics have argued that each story had serious weaknesses—one failing to stress the "official prayer" and the other failing to specify the "establishment" clause.[12]

It then becomes essential to look at the later stories as revised by wire service reporters and editors:

1:39 P.M.—First Lead:
Washington, June 25 (AP)—The Supreme Court ruled 6–1 today that New York State sponsorship of a 22–word daily prayer for recitation in public schools violates the U.S. Constitution. . . .

12:29 P.M.—First Lead:
Washington, June 25 (UPI)—The Supreme Court ruled today that the daily recital of an official state prayer in public schools is unconstitutional because it violates the religious freedom guaranteed in the Bill of Rights. . . .

And 1:18 P.M.—Second Lead:
Washington, June 25 (UPI)—The Supreme Court ruled today that it is unconstitutional to have public school children recite official state prayers as a daily exercise. . . .

It is important to stress here that the 11:54 and 11:58 stories were written in advance—with alternative leads ready to be sent out the moment the Court released the outcome. The 1:39 P.M. AP "first lead" (1 hour, 45 minutes later) and the 12:29 P.M. UPI "first lead" (31 minutes later) were written with the full opinions in hand.

The practice of sending out "new leads" is common in wire service work as part of the aim of achieving as fast news dissemination as possible. The practice not only attempts to give a running account but also provides editors with the chance to pull things together—allowing for clarification and new emphasis. News reporters at the Court, thus, often have the multiple juggling act of trying to add information while also trying to rework the main news story.

For purposes of contrast, it is helpful to note the next-day story by Anthony Lewis in the *New York Times:*

Washington, June 25—The Supreme Court held today that the reading of an official prayer in New York public schools violated the Constitution.

12. Especially noted by Hachten and Newland.

The prayer was drafted by the New York Board of Regents and recommended in 1951 for recital aloud by teachers and children in each classroom at the start of every school day. . . .

The obvious stress is on the state sponsorship—certainly an angle to be expected in a New York City newspaper. But even allowing for this advantage and the advantages of time in assembling and editing the story, it is clear by comparison that the wire services did not emphasize as much this narrow part of the Court's ruling.

Another major difference can be found in attention to public reaction. Although the *Times* and other papers did include many comments from supporters and critics of the decision, the wire services put special stress on public comment. Within an hour or so of the decision, Congressmen and religious leaders were being quoted—mostly in heated criticism of the Court's decision.

News accounts of the 1963 *Schempp* decision, in contrast, turned up no significant controversy or stress on public reaction. The fact that the following stories "don't show much" is important in itself.

The Supreme Court ruled 8 to 1 Monday that use of the Lord's Prayer and Bible reading in public schools is unconstitutional.
It held that the state must be neutral in the relationship between Man and God. . . .[13]

The Supreme Court Monday banned Bible reading and recital of the Lord's Prayer in public schools as part of required classroom exercise.
Such a practice is unconstitutional, it said in an 8-to-1 ruling on cases from Maryland and Pennsylvania. The decision also would apply in many other states where such customs are followed as part of school-day opening exercises. . . .[14]

Analysis of similar stories showed some attempted emphasis on the significance of the decision and also early mention of the 1962 ruling. While some criticisms might be made about exact wording of these lead paragraphs, they do not present the major problems of perspective evidenced in the 1962 case. One main reason is that the 1962 decision involved a relatively little-known state school prayer

13. Combined wire services story in the *Chicago Daily News*, June 17, 1963.
14. Associated Press story in the (Madison) *Wisconsin State Journal*, June 18, 1963.

while the 1963 decision involved Bible reading and the familiar Lord's Prayer.

The combined effect of subject matter and the need for care in phrasing can perhaps be best reflected in headlines. On June 26, 1962, for example, the *Chicago Sun-Times* ran the headline: "Ban Prayers in Public Schools." On June 18, 1963, its headline was: "Court Bars Reading of Bible in Schools." In the first case, of course, not all prayers were banned. In the second, while not all Bible reading was banned, there was not the same potential for gross misinterpretation.

In retrospect, there does seem to be quite a difference between headlines saying "Supreme Court Outlaws Official School Prayers in Regents Case Decision" or "School Recital of State Prayer Ruled Violation of Constitution" and "No Praying in Schools, Court Rules," or "Supreme Court Rules Prayers in Public Schools Illegal." [15]

Distinction between one prayer and all prayers was important because an individual's reaction to the decision could easily have depended on his feeling about the scope of the decision. Although the *Engel* ruling was actually narrow, the impression could easily have been that it was broad. By contrast, while the ban on devotional Bible reading and the Lord's Prayer were fairly sweeping, there was little doubt left about what the Court had ruled. Although the decision might not have been liked any more by the public official or private citizen, he could at least get a fairly firm grasp of the issues.

Evaluation and Implication

One reason why the mass media consumer did not have to wrestle as much with the 1963 decision would seem to be, indeed, because the press coverage was "better." [16] Analysis of the two decisions (especially wire service leads and headlines) leads to the conclusion that at minimum the *Schempp* coverage was adequate and at minimum the *Engel* coverage was inadequate.

15. From, in sequence: the *New York Times* and *Wisconsin State Journal*, both June 26, 1962; *Indianapolis News*, June 25, 1962; and *Congressional Quarterly Weekly Review*, June 29, 1962, p. 1106.

16. Among those noting the improvement: Justice Clark, June 10, 1965 (interview), and Judge Irving R. Kaufman, "The Supreme Court and Its Critics," *The Atlantic*, December, 1963, p. 50.

Because of the many factors at work—such as the settings of the decisions, their subject matter, and the justices' opinion-writing—it is hard to assess press responsibility for the uproar caused by the earlier decision. But, again at minimum, it would seem that the press was one element in the *Engel* case.

In the press's favor, it is important to stress that some attacks on its coverage do not turn out to be justified. There are factors that press critics have either deliberately or unintentionally overlooked.

For example, it is unfair to say that news reports of the *Engel* case reflected any special bias. There were many anti-Court reactions carried by the news media, but such a situation would be expected because those most upset by the Court's decision would tend to be most vocal. The press did try to get a variety of reactions but it could not—and should not—try to balance every negative comment with a positive one.

Also, while the key elements of the establishment clause and a state-sponsored prayer were perhaps inadequately stressed in the early coverage, these elements were not totally missing. The stories sent out on the decision were generally complete—if not always properly focused.[17] Thus, in many ways Charlotte Moulton of UPI and Paul Yost of AP were correct in saying that they had the story essentially right.[18] They felt they had done their job and that other factors had caused the confusion. Both Miss Moulton and Yost felt the religious nature of the decision was what caused a lot of people to get excited; Miss Moulton, in particular, felt that many people were "reading into" the news reports certain inaccuracies.

There is also evidence to support Julius Frandsen, UPI Washington bureau manager, in saying that critics of the press were partly con-

17. One dramatic example of incompleteness, however, might be the following NBC radio news item at 2 P.M. on the decision day: "The Supreme Court—in a far-reaching decision—has ruled as unconstitutional the recitation by public school children of an official state prayer in New York State classrooms. The 6-1 decision cited the concept of church and state." (*Columbia Journalism Review*, Winter, 1963, p. 54.) This excessive brevity reflects one staggering problem for radio and television news: being able to give only highlights on even major stories.

18. These comments are based on remarks quoting Yost and Miss Moulton in *Editor & Publisher*, Aug. 11, 1962, p. 11; and on a personal interview with Miss Moulton, May 7, 1965.

fusing what news agencies had written with what members of Congress or the clergy were saying.[19]

Law Professor Paul Freund is among those who tended to agree that the real problem was reaction by public officials. From a transcript of the CBS program "Storm Over the Supreme Court," came this interview:

> Eric Sevareid: Professor Freund, what about the press handling of this religious case in the schools? Associate Justice Clark said he thought it was rather badly presented.
> Paul Freund: Justice Clark evidently spoke under great provocation. I think the immediate reporting of the decision by the news services was not inaccurate, or a distortion, given the pressure of time and the limitations of space of the wire services, and the newscasting. I think the real problem is the interpretation of the opinions in editorial comment, and in the publicized comment of public figures. . . .[20]

Evidence is that the press did become preoccupied with the public furor. The actual decision of the Court was overpowered by public commentary in the press and the pouring out of all kinds of responsible and irresponsible comments. (For example, suggestions were made to impeach Earl Warren—in some cases by people who had obviously not even read the Court's opinion.) Professor Philip Kurland's reaction was:

> What they [newspapers] did was to solicit, at the time that public opinion was being formulated, the opinions of people, many of whom were not even in the country, the very afternoon the Supreme Court decision came down. Theoretically they informed these people what the result was and asked for their comment about whether they thought it was a good idea and the obvious result came forth. . . .[21]

The implications of such a transmission role on the part of the press are so far-reaching as to need more discussion and evaluation later. But, clearly, the press must take considerable responsibility for so actively seeking out the "good quotes" and colorful reactions without much regard for validity. The press can sometimes build a defense

19. *Editor & Publisher*, Aug. 11, 1962; and interview with Frandsen, May 19, 1965.

20. Part Two, "The School Prayer Case," March 13, 1963, transcript, p. 69.

21. U.S. House of Representatives, Hearings before the Committee on the Judiciary, May 27, 1964, p. 2153.

by arguing that its role is not to pass judgment on the comments of others, but it is on shaky ground even here because some of its own members were caught up in the uninformed and emotional distortion. For example, the reaction of columnist George E. Sokolsky:

> The Supreme Court, having voted 6–1 to eliminate God from the public schools, may have taken the joy out of the lives of children by removing religious holidays which are so meaningful. . . .
> Mr. Justice Black and his five supporters in the Supreme Court have apparently no sense of tradition and history.[22]

Or perhaps even more devastating was a widely distributed editorial cartoon showing a Lincoln penny and the robed arm of a man with a chisel and gavel in his hands. From the words "In God We Trust" on the penny, the letters G—O—D are being dramatically chipped away.[23]

There are also other elements, besides interpretation, in the *Engel* case which show the performance of the press as less than adequate. In particular, *Brown Shoe Co.* v. *U.S.*, another decision on that day and one which observers of the Court feel was fairly important, was generally neglected by the wire services and newspapers around the country. While it can be argued that the flood of news on that decision day was too great, such an excuse does not meet the point that the job of the press is to cover all the news. If manpower was inadequate to cover all Court cases that day, then the manpower should have been increased.

To argue that part of the problem that day was due to the fact that stories had been prepared in advance is, of course, also no defense at all. If the prepared story failed to tell what it should tell, then it should have been rewritten. Here, the wire services' self-imposed preoccupation with speed obviously affected the content of the early news product.

It also seems unsatisfactory for any news media to argue that the term "establishment" was too complicated for the average reader to understand and thus was not worth explaining at any length. To

---

22. The *Washington Post*, July 7, 1962.
23. Burris Jenkins, Jr., *New York Journal-American*, reprinted in Hachten, "Journalism and the Prayer Decision," p. 8.

say there was not space to define establishment avoids the counter-argument that the concept was so basic to the news event that to neglect it was to bypass an essential part of the news happening.

Ironically, there is still another area in which sectors of the press fell down in their duties. The news media pride themselves on their speed of information dissemination, yet both haste and depth in reporting were generally absent during the confusing period after the decision. For example, an interpretative article by Raymond Crow for the Associated Press was not sent out until July 2, a week after the decision was announced. A United Press International analysis by Louis Cassels, also helpful in perspective, was sent out roughly ten days after the decision. There were other efforts, but absent was any full-fledged drive by the wire services, especially, to speed their clarifications.

Reasons for such heel-dragging are multiple but fairly easy to trace. Follow-up stories admitting confusion or even errors are not very good news items. They are embarrassing and certainly do not help sell papers or build public confidence in a news organization. It is much easier to follow the built-in story of public furor, letting public figures and private citizens argue the case.

In sum, with the advantage of hindsight, it is obvious that the *Engel* case required extra care, if necessary at the sacrifice of speed. The decision was too difficult to treat like most others. When the public confusion did evolve, parts of the press should have taken a more active role in trying to clarify exactly what had happened and what it meant.

If the press's obligation is to provide more than just a flood of facts and comments, then much of the news coverage of the *Engel* decision failed to meet a demanding standard of adequacy. The press can often get by with this type of coverage; but in this unusual and dramatic situation in 1962, it is significant that the media were caught by even the slightest of failings, limitations, or bad habits. By contrast, in 1963, the setting had changed enough and the participants were ready enough so that the news coverage was much improved.

A PRIZE-WINNING EFFORT AND ONE THAT FELL SHORT

Reapportionment

On May 6, 1963, Anthony Lewis of the *New York Times* was awarded a Pulitzer Prize for "distinguished reporting of the proceedings of the United States Supreme Court during the year [1962] with particular emphasis on the coverage of the decision in the reapportionment case and its consequences in many of the states of the union." [24]

Baker v. *Carr*, decided March 26, 1962, ranks as one of the most important Court decisions in recent history. For this reason alone, it is worth brief examination in terms of press coverage. But perhaps most important is the fact that the prize-winning nature of the coverage tells as much about the *Times's* approaches to news as it does about Lewis' work. Without implying that all Court newsmen could or should try to imitate the *Times*, this summary analysis does point out what the press can do when full manpower and other resources are put to work.

It is important to note that the case was a complex one, involving considerable in-fighting among members of the Court. As Justice Clark observed in his concurring opinion: "One emerging from the rash of opinions with their accompanying clashing of views may well find himself suffering from a mental blindness. . . ." Or, as Justice Stewart noted: "The separate writings of my dissenting and concurring Brothers stray so far from the subject of today's decision as to convey, I think, a distressingly inaccurate impression of what the Court decides. . . ." With this to contend with, Lewis wrote in his lead story on page 1 of the March 27, 1962, *Times:*

> WASHINGTON, March 26—The Supreme Court held today that the distribution of seats in State Legislatures was subject to the constitutional scrutiny of the Federal courts.
>
> The historic decision was a sharp departure from the court's traditional reluctance to get into questions of fairness in legislative districting. It could significantly affect the nation-wide struggle of urban, rural and suburban forces for political power.
>
> The vote, in a case brought by Tennessee city-dwellers, was 6 to 2.

24. Quoted in the *New York Times*, May 7, 1963.

Justice William J. Brennan, Jr., wrote the opinion of the court, joined by Chief Justice Earl Warren and Justices Hugo L. Black, William O. Douglas, Tom C. Clark and Potter Stewart. Justices Douglas, Clark and Stewart also wrote separate concurring opinions.

The dissenters—each joining in an opinion by the other—were Justices Felix Frankfurter and John Marshall Harlan. Justice Charles E. Whittaker, who has been in the hospital ten days for a physical check-up, took no part in the decision.

Summary of Decision

The Supreme Court's action was only a first step into the apportionment field. It left many questions for decision later. In summary, today's decision did the following:

It held that the Federal courts had the power, and the duty, to consider the constitutionality of state legislative apportionments.

It said that some apportionments could be so unfair as to violate the clause of the Fourteenth Amendment providing that *no* state shall "deny to any person . . . the equal protection of the laws."

It refused at this time to indicate how bad an apportionment would have to be before it was deemed unconstitutional.

While only Tennessee's legislative districts were under attack in the case decided today, many states will probably be forced, as a result, to defend the validity of their apportionment in court. . . .

Lewis' story then carried over to page 19 and went on for another 30 column inches, or roughly three times more than the amount of this 10-paragraph opening passage.

Other summary statistics of the coverage are significant. The *Times* carried more than 1½ full inside pages of excerpts from the Court's opinions, or roughly another 250 column inches of type. In addition, under the main four-column headline on page 1, it carried two related stories: one an interpretative article from Washington by James Reston, and the other a New York State-angle story from Albany. Together, these two articles ran on page 1 and inside for about 50 column inches. Added to these were: a 20-column-inch background story on page 20 and another 24-column-inch story from Nashville, Tennessee; a roughly 8-column-inch table showing decline in urban representation in Tennessee; half a dozen one-column pictures of the justices; and an editorial page column by Arthur Krock.

All this added up, including headlines, to more than 450 column inches of space, or roughly the equivalent of three full pages of type, pictures, and headlines. Based on roughly 150 lines of type in a full inside page column of the *Times* and 4–5 words per line, more than 14,000 words were carried on the one case. Of the 400 total column inches, roughly 250 came from reprinting parts of the Court's opinions. But this still left 5,000–5,500 words written by *Times* staff—of which most were pounded out on typewriters within only 5 to 10 hours.

It does not take away from Lewis' effort to point out that he had a lot of help and that such "blanket coverage" by the *Times* has been common on many major Court decision days.[25] But it is important to note how much the scope of the *Times* helped Lewis cover the reapportionment case. Teamwork eased his burden; he was able to concentrate primarily on the main page 1 news story.

The following analysis of the main story does not imply that it was "perfect" or that it could not have been improved. But it is especially meaningful to note several of the strong points. In particular, Lewis was able to give both factual information on what happened and factual interpretation of what happened. He was able to give the story both detailed short-term and long-term perspective—partly because he was "freed" to do so but also partly because he was not "afraid" to do so. Lewis clearly was not scared to put himself on the spot; he was willing to write as the supposedly informed Court observer and interpreter.

Lewis' news story organization stressed highlights and summaries and left most of the specific quotes from the opinion for the pages of partial texts. In contrast to wire service coverage which tended to stress quotes by the justices early in the news stories, Lewis was able to give more and sooner attention to interpretation. He took the initiative of trying to make clear what the Court meant, rather than falling back on the easier approach of letting the justices try to say things in their own words. Although the *Times*'s philosophy is clearly an effort to record "instant history," it is especially significant that Lewis' approach was also to try to provide instant "interpretative history." He knew that the exact words of the justices could be carried elsewhere in his paper.

In sum, this *Times* coverage shows what can be done under optimum conditions. To say that these resources are available, however, does

25. For another example, see the *Times's* June 13, 1967, coverage of the Court's last day which included five separate page 1 stories and a total of four bylined articles throughout the paper, written by four different reporters.

not necessarily mean that an outstanding or good job will be done. It just happens in this situation that Lewis and the *Times* responded to history in the making by doing the job expected of them—and a little bit more.

Miranda

On June 14, 1966, the *New York Times* gave its major headline of the day to *Miranda* v. *Arizona*—one of the celebrated cases in the series of Court decisions restricting police powers in interrogation of suspects. Under a bylined story by Fred P. Graham, the article began:

> WASHINGTON, June 13—The Supreme Court announced today sweeping limitations on the power of the police to question suspects in their custody.
> The Justices split 5 to 4. In stinging dissents the minority denounced the decision as helping criminals go free to repeat their crimes.
> The majority opinion, by Chief Justice Earl Warren, broke new constitutional ground by declaring that the Fifth Amendment's privilege against self-incrimination comes into play as soon as a person is within police custody.
> Under the ruling, the prosecution cannot use in a trial any admissions or confessions made by the suspect while in custody unless it first proves that the police complied with a detailed list of safeguards to protect the right against self-incrimination. . . .

The rest of the *Times* story and coverage continued the pattern of its usual major decision-day coverage—with lengthy excerpts from the justices' opinions and with several news analyses and other reaction stories. In total, *Times* editors gave about two-thirds the amount of coverage to *Miranda* as it had to the 1962 *Baker* v. *Carr* reapportionment case—still a healthy 9,000–plus words, including about 6,500 words of text from the majority and dissenting opinions.

But, as Des Moines editorial writer Gilbert Cranberg pointed out, the Court's *Miranda* decision totaled more than 37,000 words.[26]

26. Main source used here: Cranberg's "What Did the Supreme Court Say?" *Saturday Review*, April 8, 1967, pp. 90–92. For one study of other criminal procedure cases over time, see Russell Wheeler, "Chicago Press Coverage of the U.S. Supreme Court: How the Criminal Procedure Revolution from Mapp to Miranda was reported in the Chicago Press" (Final version of Master's thesis, University of Chicago, 1968).

Missing from the *Times*'s coverage was the extensive quotation in Chief Justice Warren's opinion from manuals used to instruct the police in the techniques of interrogation. The opinion pointed out that the manuals had been used widely by law enforcement agencies and then went on to cite sections from them. Perhaps the most revealing was the section offering advice from a lecturer in police science:

> In the preceding paragraphs emphasis has been placed on kindness and strategems. The investigator will, however, encounter many situations where the sheer weight of his personality will be the deciding factor. Where emotional appeals and tricks are employed to no avail, he must rely on an oppressive atmosphere of dogged persistence. He must interrogate steadily and without relent, leaving the subject no prospect of surcease. He must dominate his subject and overwhelm him with his inexorable will to obtain the truth. He should interrogate for a spell of several hours pausing only for the subject's necessities in acknowledgment of the need to avoid a charge of duress that can be technically substantiated. In a serious case, the interrogation may continue for days, with the required intervals for food and sleep, but with no respite from the atmosphere of domination. It is possible in this way to induce the subject to talk without resorting to duress or coercion. This method should be used only when the guilt of the suspect appears highly probable.[27]

Cranberg concluded:

> The *Times* dealt comprehensively and accurately with *what* the Court decided in regard to the police warnings that must be given to suspects, but its usually well-informed readers were less adequately informed about *why* the Court concluded that warnings are essential. The outcry that followed the Court's *Miranda* ruling might have been less piercing if there had been more general public awareness of the nature of the interrogation evils the Court sought to combat and took the trouble to cite at length.[28]

It would seem that parts of the *why* were missing in the *Times*'s *Miranda* coverage—as they were in the New York Regents prayer case coverage in 1962 when the paper (interestingly, much to the surprise of several lawyers interviewed) also missed carrying Justice Black's famous footnote 21. A good case can be built in saying that the Court should not bury such elements or should be more careful to

27. 384 U.S. 436, 451 (1966).
28. "What Did the Supreme Court Say?" p. 91.

point them out. Yet, despite this partial escape, the fact remains that news media are supposed to be able to dig out all crucial why's and explanations. Even with all the resources and talents available, the *Times* formula simply does not always work as well as it could and should. It is hard to blame the *Times* for any possible public confusion caused by the *Miranda* case; but, as with the wire services' coverage of the 1962 school prayer decision, the evidence is clearly that the *Times* did not make the decision fully meaningful. The paper's news reporting job obviously was not to try to sell the majority's reasoning or to be at all concerned about how good or bad a decision was being handed down. But, as with any news event, part of the press's obligation was to provide perspective as to what exactly had gone into the event.

CRITICAL ANALYSIS OF OTHER SELECTED AND REPRESENTATIVE COURT DECISIONS: 1965–67

Detailed analysis of Court decisions during the term of the Supreme Court ending June, 1965, was made in an effort to get at typical types of news coverage problems. Although examples of articles from the 1965/66 and 1966/67 terms of the Court have been added, the bulk of examination and conclusion-drawing is based upon an intensive period of case study in Washington during April, May, and June, 1965. The purpose was to try to get away from the most unusual news situations and to look at the more representative coverage on a long-term basis. News items, articles, and columns cited are a mixture of purposively and randomly selected cases. (Details on methodology are outlined in Appendix A.)

Types of Problems Reflected

One important variable in any news story produced is the nature of the event involved. The difference between relatively easy Court decisions and complicated ones can be dramatically illustrated by two minor items that appeared in succession in the *Washington Post*, tacked on to a longer article on the Court:[29]

29. April 27, 1965, p. 2.

The Supreme Court refused to review a ruling under which a
Chicago lawyer, Austin L. Wyman, Jr., was held to a fee of $250
for representing an indigent who was acquitted of murder.

The $250 fee is the maximum allowed under an Illinois law that the
State Supreme Court ruled Wyman lacked standing to challenge. The
trial court had allowed him $1,500. He calculated that at usual rates
he and an associate were owed $8,983.

There are obvious questions that could be asked, but the essence
of the story seems to be here. In contrast is the item that followed:

In what one Justice called a landmark decision, the Court held in
essence that Federal Rules of Civil Procedure must prevail when there
is a conflict with state law about how summonses and complaints will
be served in so-called diversity actions.

In these cases, Federal Courts have jurisdiction because the op-
posing parties reside in different states. The decision reversed the
First Circuit Court of Appeals in an auto accident suit filed in Massa-
chusetts.

Just as obvious here are the many questions left unanswered. The
story needs several readings before it starts to become clear. But
even then the lay reader faces such crucial obstacles as: what are the
Federal Rules of Civil Procedure? It is doubtful that even the parties
involved in the automobile accident would know for sure that the
case was about them. About all this news story can do is to alert those
especially interested to the fact that a certain type of case was decided
on a certain date. Little information and even less understanding
is conveyed. Anyone really interested would have to turn to the full
written opinion and record laid out before the Court.

Part of the contrast here may come from the way the two stories
were written. But certainly the latter story was not conducive to
handling in two paragraphs, while the former generally was.

The problem of the too brief story is common throughout news
work because of the struggle for time and space. For example, an
early afternoon home delivery edition of the June 12, 1967, *Chicago
Daily News*, carried a 10-inch story on Dr. Martin Luther King's
conviction (for a civil rights demonstration) that was upheld by the
Supreme Court. Besides barely touching on the real legal issues,
2½ inches of the story tried also to report the following:

In other actions the court:
Struck down in a unanimous decision Virginia's—and by implica-

tion 15 other states'—laws making interracial marriage a crime.

Set aside former Maj. Gen. Edwin A. Walker's $500,000 libe [sic] judgment against the Associated Press.

Declared unconstitutional a New York tate [sic] law permitting court-approved electronic eavesdropping in criminal cases.

It might be argued that most readers would not want the details of these three cases. For many this might be true, but obviously for some such coverage would be totally inadequate. (It also is intriguing that the story from "Daily News Wire Services" mentioned General Walker's libel case but totally ignored the Court's decision upholding a libel judgment against the *Saturday Evening Post*. Extensive news media coverage was given the *Post* case across the country, but editors at the *Daily News* apparently felt it did not merit much attention for early editions.)

Closely related to the problem of the too brief story is the too vague one. Often the two go together, with the excessive brevity usually affecting the clarity. But sometimes there are news stories that, although given enough space, just do not come through clearly. Such may be the case when the reporter either does not have enough exact information, deliberately tries to save space by leaving out elements, or perhaps is even trying unintentionally to "skim the surface" of the story because it is really easier to write hurriedly that way.

An effective example of this vagueness problem was a wire service story, April 27, 1965, in the *Washington Post* on oral arguments in the Communist mail case (*Lamont* v. *Postmaster General*).[30] The notes in parentheses following each paragraph are some of the unanswered questions that a curious lawyer, public official, or layman might well be tempted to ask.

> The Supreme Court heard arguments yesterday challenging a 1962 law that permits the Postmaster General to destroy alleged Communist political propaganda mail unless the addressee asks for it.

(What happened to the arguments defending the law? Weren't they heard, too?)

30. At the time the article was clipped and first analyzed it was not known that this decision would be part of the diary analysis of Dana Bullen's (May 24) coverage in the *Washington Evening Star*.

The law violates the Constitution and is an interference "with the tradition of an open society," said an attorney representing Corliss Lamont, a New York pamphlet publisher.

(How does this violate the Constitution? Isn't Corliss Lamont known as someone more important than just a "pamphlet publisher"?)

Lamont's case and an appeal from the decision in a three-judge Federal court in San Francisco calling the law "unconstitutional on its face" were heard jointly in a two-hour oral argument before the high court. A Federal court in New York has ruled the Lamont case moot, that is, no longer an issue.

(Why are there two cases? There are many levels of Federal courts —which are involved here? It is helpful to have "moot" explained, but why did the judge rule the case was moot? What happened?)

The issues of freedom of speech and press were raised in arguments challenging the law. It requires the Post Office to notify the recipient of unsealed foreign mail that has been determined to be "Communist political propaganda" that it will be forwarded to him if he requests. Otherwise it will be destroyed.

(What, specifically, are the "issues of freedom of speech and press"? Where did the foreign angle come from? The lead paragraph didn't mention this—is it an essential issue? How does the Post Office determine what is or isn't "Communist political propaganda"? Is this determination at issue? How much time does the addressee have to notify the Post Office? How does he do it?)

Solicitor General Archibald Cox said the law protects some people who don't want unsolicited Communist propaganda dropped on their doorstep where "nosy neighbors are going to draw the wrong inference from it." But he conceded that the open postcard the Post Office sent asking the resident whether he wanted to accept certain Communist literature also could promote gossip.

(The Solicitor General represents the Federal government as the other part in this case?)

Among the issues raised was the question of whether a "black book" list, as Chief Justice Earl Warren referred to it, is being kept by the Post Office or Customs officiials [sic] on those who request the Communist literature.

(Well, is it?)

Questioning by Justice Arthur J. Goldberg brought out that such publications as the New York Times or the Times of London, or such a noted personality as Bertrand Russell, might at times have their publications subjected to these "Communist political propaganda" regulations if they were to reprint material or speeches considered prepared on behalf of Communist countries.

(What is the significance of this? Would the "at times" mean any time that material was reprinted? Does "reprinted" mean as news stories? Would this mean any time a Communist speech is reported? The foreign angle seems important here again—is it?)

Each critic of this article could devise his own variations of this running commentary, including the point that the article over-all seems weighted against the Post Office practice. But the main point is that this story, even though seven paragraphs long, does not adequately explain the news event. Not all of the questions raised here are important or could be answered well in the space allotted, but it would seem that either the reporter did not "do his homework" or was attempting to "write it off quickly" and to get on to some other task. The result was a news story adequate in many ways in telling what happened but inadequate in the sharpness of focus, perspective, and clarity needed to convey high levels of meaning to the reader.

In many ways such coverage of oral arguments is most like news in other government fields because the conflicting issues get vivid exposure (like a legislative debate) during those one or two hours in the courtroom.

By contrast, however, there is perhaps no more difficult story in which to get at the why's of a decision than that of a very brief Court order denying to hear a case. The reasons usually are not given. The result is that sometimes the reporter is forced to struggle with very speculative interpretation. Usually such efforts are cautious in tone, using vague phrasing such as: the Court "declined to take up" the issue "at this time" through a "brief, unsigned order."

One reason for such limited press interpretation may well date back to the classic error in the 1956 South Carolina bus segregation case, which, instead of being a decision of great significance (banning racial segregation on buses), turned out only to be a case where the

Court refused to consider an appeal because there had not been a final judgment in a trial court.[31]

It took several days for the press to straighten out its mistake.[32] But, to this day, newsmen are still at least semi-aware of the trouble caused by that 1956 Court order which read only: "No. 511 South Carolina Electric and Gas Co. v. Flemming. Per curiam, the appeal is dismissed. Shaker v. O'Connor. 278 U.S. 188."

Besides the fear of misinterpretation, there is also the problem of appropriateness in any interpretation of certiorari. The law is what is written and the reasons, if not noted, are then, in a sense, not part of the news event. The Court newsman, thus, does face unique limitations in trying to explain the why's of such governmental decisions.

Ironically, however, sometimes the news media go far in the other direction in interpretation and speculation on such "non-legal matters" as the presidential appointment of a new justice. For example, when Justice Goldberg resigned in 1965 to take the job as United States Ambassador to the United Nations, all of a sudden columnists and newsmen around the country became "experts" on who might be appointed as his successor. Abe Fortas, who finally was named, was among those mentioned, but he was literally only one among scores. It is especially interesting that few of the regular or even semi-regular reporters around the Court joined in the game of "name the justice." It was, instead, mostly the columnists or political and White House reporters who became so speculative.

Perhaps the most far-out example was a July 21, 1965, story by Jack Bell of the Associated Press which indicated that the President was about to appoint either a Negro or a woman—or, better, yet, a Negro woman. The *Washington Evening Star* was among the papers that carried the Bell story in early editions and then yanked most of it out of later editions after the White House had publicly criticized the press for letting its speculation get out of hand.[33]

---

31. Details here are from especially: Robert U. Brown, "Shop Talk at Thirty," *Editor & Publisher*, May 12, 1956, p. 90; and James E. Clayton, "News from the Supreme Court and Justice Department," in Ray E. Hiebert (ed.), *The Press in Washington* (New York: Dodd, Mead and Co., 1966), pp. 182–84.

32. See, for example, the *New York Times's* awkwardly indirect admission of error and effort to clarify what had been decided in an article by Luther A. Huston, Wednesday, April 25, 1956.

33. One extensive news story on the criticism can be found in the *Washington Post*, July 22, 1965.

The 1967 appointment of Solicitor General Thurgood Marshall, a Negro, shows that such speculation was not as far off as some might have said it was at the time. Yet, name-dropping to the point of suggesting a "Negro woman" for the Court, did not seem probable enough to warrant such emphasis. It is also interesting to note that some columnists and political experts were again among the first to evaluate the President's choice of Marshall and to speculate on what his selection would mean for the internal balance of the Court.[34]

In contrast with a seemingly careful effort by the *Times*'s Fred P. Graham to analyze the significance of the appointment,[35] much of the interpretation immediately following the announcement would have to be rated as mostly superficial, not very informed, and unsophisticated. Most of the attention was preoccupied with the "Negro angle" and what it might mean for civil rights decisions, but little depth or solid information was usually provided on Marshall's legal experience and his background in other areas.

In defense of the press, it should be noted that it is hard to speculate about an appointee's likely legal direction once he gets on the Court. In fact, the history of the Court is full of surprises—supposed liberals who turned out to be legal conservatives and vice versa. In addition, to complicate things further, a "liberal" on civil rights matters (such as Justice Fortas) may not be a "liberal" at all on labor-management or obscenity questions.

Indeed, the newsman at the Court shares a common problem with his colleagues covering the Capitol or White House and any state capitol or governor's mansion in the country: the danger of labels. Regular reporters at the Court usually try to avoid sweeping categorizations as to judicial thinking. Thus, Justice Black, becomes a "liberal"—but, especially in recent years, only sometimes and on certain issues. Whether a reader or listener would grasp this subtle distinction would depend on the writer's expertise in the Court and care in language.

The dangers of labeling and oversimplification haunt most newsmen in most news work; but in writing about the Court, the po-

34. See, for example, the syndicated column by Joseph Kraft, "LBJ's Court Choice Not 'Best' Possible," *Chicago Daily News*, June 16, 1967.
35. "Marshall's Meaning for the Court," *New York Times Week in Review*, June 18, 1967.

tential for this pitfall appears great, especially among columnists and editorial writers trying to make black-and-white judgments on judicial reasoning in only a few hundred words. In trying to translate a Court ruling (with perhaps limited knowledge of the subject), the editorial writer or columnist often tries to reduce a complex issue to a simple one. As one example, after the 1966 *Miranda* decision, the *Chicago Tribune* editorialized on June 14, 1966, under the heading, "Why Police Get Gray":

> A divided decision by the Supreme court [sic] yesterday makes it ever more difficult to hang a conviction on a criminal defendant. Taken in conjunction with a long series of previous holdings by the court, the decision throws up another roadblock in the path of police and prosecutors.

The point is not that the *Tribune* is right or wrong in its interpretation but that such sweeping phrases tend to be misleading, or at least confuse the real issues. The same holds true for the *Tribune*'s conclusion:

> Yesterday Justice White and his dissenting colleagues found themselves hollering down the Old Warren rain barrel, while the majority, in Justice Black's characterization of a year ago, continued blithely to sit as "a day-to-day constitutional convention."

Equally misleading statements are, of course, often made in pro-Court articles and columns.[36] But, again, analytical concern here is not with the ideology but with the lack of solid perspective provided for the reader. While it can be argued that glittering and sweeping generalities and selective choice of words are expected and fair game in editorials and opinion columns, such a defense cannot be effectively used for occasional articles on the Court that—under the guise of analysis—take very biased positions.

It is certainly true that the news media have gone a long way in reducing bias since the time that the *New York Herald Tribune* wrote the following about Chief Justice Roger Taney's opinion in the famed *Dred Scott* case:

36. Perhaps one of the best recent examples of seemingly excessive and "semi-distorted" praise: Fred Rodell, "It Is the Earl Warren Court," the *New York Times Magazine*, March 13, 1966, pp. 30–31, and 93–100.

. . . of Taney's opinion, it will be found to exhibit all the characteristics that have marked his career. It is subtle, ingenious, sophistical and false. It is the plea of a tricky lawyer and not the decree of an upright Judge. It is a singular, but not wonderful fact in nature, that the body to some extent intimates the character of the soul that inhabits it. This is the case with Judge Taney. He walks with inverted and hesitating steps. His forehead is contracted, his eye sunken and his visage has a sinister expression.[37]

But despite the obvious toning down and reduced slanting in news columns, there still are mass media organizations that seem to enjoy slipping in their subtle and not-too-subtle attacks on the Court.[38] While it may help the perspective of the reader to know that some people passionately feel that the Court has been "totally out of bounds" or is "violating the faith of our founding fathers," such subjective judgments only serve to reinforce existing reader biases and do not communicate much understanding and awareness of the Court's strengths and weaknesses.

Thus, perhaps noticeable as one major problem in much media coverage is the "quickness to judge" Court decisions seemingly without an understanding of all the issues or without the willingness to show the issues as usually gray rather than black and white.

A Sampling of Decision Days

It is relatively easy to look back for selected specific examples of press coverage problems, but one obvious danger may be to distort the patterns of over-all performance. In an effort to get at a more systematic and representative analysis of cases, three decision days— May 24, June 1, and June 7, 1965—were selected in advance to be studied. The first two days' analysis concentrated on wire service coverage combined with some comparisons of purposively selected news-

37. Quoted in Charles Warren, *The Supreme Court in U.S. History* (Boston: Little, Brown & Co., 1935), II: 319. It is especially interesting that the historian Warren felt that the press played a major part in misleading the country about the *Dred Scott* decision and especially about Chief Justice Taney's role in it (see pp. 303–4 and 317–19).

38. For two excellent recent examples see: "How Supreme Court Is Changing U.S." *U.S. News & World Report,* Jan. 18, 1965, especially pp. 56–57; and Eugene H. Methvin, "Is the Supreme Court Really Supreme?" *Reader's Digest,* July, 1967, pp. 80–85.

papers; the June 7 analysis concentrated on the coverage of 12 randomly selected daily newspapers. From this random sampling came a related later study that combined analysis of headline coverage of the 1965 Estes television-in-the-courtroom case with the 1966 Dr. Sam Sheppard free press-fair trial decision.[39]

The May 24 and June 1 decision days turned out to be quite different in the patterns of news coverage. As noted in the diary analysis of Dana Bullen's work at the *Washington Evening Star*, the Communist mail case turned out to be the single "big story" on May 24. Both the wire services led with this item, as did such newspapers as the *New York Times* and *Washington Post*. There was a high level of agreement among the news regulars as to what the major story was.

But May 24 was also unusual in that it included the special feature of the nun being sworn in (as a lawyer) before the Court. One of the wire services did get the picture of the nun standing with her sponsor, Senator Hart from Michigan. It was ironic that some papers gave the event almost as much space as the Communist mail case.[40] Here, clearly, was a "natural story" that met one basic standard of news selection: "the unusual with human interest." The nun story is also significant in that it shows how the coverage of such an event is left primarily to the wire services. It was an example of the "stopgap" function; papers such as the *New York Times* and *Washington Evening Star* were free to use the wire services' picture and story—if they desired.

The wire service coverage of the Communist mail case was typical in stressing quotations from the justices' opinions. This concept of "formula" writing is not much different from that found in the *New York Times* or *Wall Street Journal*, but it does tend to be more regular and conspicuous and places much less emphasis on news interpretation. AP and UPI stress the "what happened," with interpretation of the what happened near the middle or end of the story where it is likely, of course, to be sliced off by some local copy editor. (Examples of

39. Methods of case selection are outlined briefly in Appendix A.
40. The *New York Times*, somewhat characteristically, buried the wire service picture on p. 19 as a one-column shot of the nun with Senator Hart cropped out. The *Washington Evening Star* gave the incident about as much inside page coverage as anyone: using both a two-column picture of the nun with Senator Hart and a roughly 12-inch wire service story.

several of the news stories analyzed here are included in Appendix B.)

Another way of saying the same thing is that the wire services tend to be quite "non-individualistic"—stressing mostly facts, with little impression left that the reporter is trying to write as an expert on the Court with his own interpretation.

An overview of the June 1 coverage shows similar patterns in wire service coverage. But decisions that day turned up some unusual news problems and some dramatically different emphases in stories.

The Court met only about ten minutes for oral announcements. But out of these few moments came a rush of Court orders denying requests to hear state appeals on legislative reapportionment. Instead of one major decision, there were actually four very separate, yet very similar decisions—one each involving New York, California, Illinois, and Idaho.

The wire services had to wrestle with each decision separately and also had to try to put them together into one single story that made sense. Meanwhile, papers in New York City or Chicago were struggling with local angles. Perhaps the best illustration was the *New York Times* coverage which gave the state decision its top play on June 2, along with an Albany-angle story, while the California, Illinois, and Idaho situations were barely mentioned in passing.

The other three major cases that day were a Federal Trade Commission and Federal Power Commission decision, a legal rights issue, and a Court order involving the murder in Georgia of a Washington, D.C., Negro school official.

The result was that while the wire services were stressing all of the reapportionment cases and the *Times* was stressing its state decision, other papers varied in what they emphasized. The *Wall Street Journal*, as would be expected, carried separate major stories on both reapportionment and the FTC-FPC decision. Meanwhile, the *Washington Post* and *Washington Evening Star* buried the "non-local" reapportionment decision on inside pages. The lead *Post* item on page 1 turned out to be the legal rights case; the Negro school official case was given 7 column inches on page A12. The *Star*, by contrast, gave the Court's decision to review the case of the murdered Negro official a banner headline across its late afternoon edition: "High Court To Review Penn Case." The legal rights story was given 10 inches on page 3.

The reasons for such patterns of coverage are partly speculative. But besides the obvious crucial geographical concerns, it would seem also that the *Post's* "liberal leanings" pushed it toward the case involving an individual's civil rights, while the *Star*, by contrast more conservative and less happy with recent efforts by the Court to protect the rights of criminals, went the "splashier" route with the major headline for the day involving the murder of a prominent local Negro. This pattern reflected the *Star's* primary interest in District of Columbia coverage. And it is a pattern common with afternoon papers which may use larger headlines and more dramatic events in an effort to increase late afternoon street sales.

In the overview of June 1 coverage it is impossible to assess whether each paper's judgment was right or wrong. What does show up dramatically, however, are the occasional great variations in emphasis that seem to be caused primarily by such obvious variables as geographic location, a news organization's self-concept of its news responsibilities, and even those "semi-subjective" personal and institutional judgments.

The final day, June 7, provided—as do nearly all final decision days each term—a variety of Court decisions. The last day is usually the busiest each year for Court newsmen, and often extra staff are assigned to help the regulars with the extra load. It is also the one day of the term when newsmen pretty well know what cases are coming up; unless a decision is postponed for rehearing in the next term, all cases left on the Court calendar must be announced. This June 7 there were seven separate or overlapping cases left and five likely stories. The two major ones were the television-in-the courtroom decision involving Billie Sol Estes and the Connecticut birth control case.[41]

June 7 turned out to be a particularly significant day. First, it was the first final day under the new policy of releasing decisions any day the Court was sitting (the number of decisions left, thus, was roughly one-half that of previous years). Second, the day turned out to coincide with the return from space of the Gemini IV astronauts. The significance of the Gemini story was that it was to grab all major head-

41. Eventually: *Estes* v. *Texas*, 381 U.S. 532, and *Griswold* v. *Connecticut*, 381 U.S. 479.

lines across the country that day and the next. The Supreme Court automatically was the number two news story—at least in the eyes of nearly all the editors throughout the country.

As things turned out, the Court day was plenty hectic. The Court handed down its first two decisions at 10:49 A.M. and 10:55 A.M. The Estes TV case came at 11:30, two labor cases together at 12:05 P.M., the birth control decision at 12:23, and a final labor case at 1 P.M. The session ended with the list of Court orders at 1:05 P.M.—only minutes before the astronauts' returning space capsule hit the ocean at 1:13 P.M.

In total, the final day resulted in twenty-one separate opinions handed out in about two hours. Two of the decisions, television-in-the-courtroom and birth control, each contained six separate majority, concurring, and dissenting opinions.

The most important resulting news pattern was the competition of the decisions for time and space in the media. For example, some observers felt the *Jewel Tea* decision handed down that day was both interesting and important and that if the decision had come on another day it likely would have received much more attention. But any decisions that day were forced to take back seats to the *Estes* and *Griswold* decisions.

The news value of Court decisions is not really judged in advance of actual announcement by the Court; but, indeed, there is considerable anticipation as to which are likely to be the "bigger stories." Although leaving themselves flexible for possible changes in priorities, Court newsmen do tend to see upcoming Court decisions in categories of likely importance. This point is especially intriguing when the significance of the final decision day is considered. Such papers as the *New York Times* reserve possible extra space for Court coverage because they know that crucial decisions are often left for the final day. (The more complex and controversial cases often simply take longer to decide; the Court clearly likes to get at least most of the less difficult decisions out of the way first.) But then an interesting question must be raised: do some cases *become* important because they are left for the final day?

Such would seem to have been partly the case with the *Estes* and *Griswold* decisions. Both the *New York Times* and *Washington Post*, for example, carried lengthy excerpts from the two decisions—a practice that is obviously a source of pride to both papers. Certainly, by comparison with other decisions during that term of the Court, the *Estes* and *Griswold* decisions were among the more important. But by comparison with other final decision days at the Court, one can only wonder whether these stories were perhaps overemphasized. Observers and scholars of the Court point out that neither decision was really an "earthshaker"; both decisions, while interesting and fairly significant legal developments, were not especially far-reaching in scope or implication.

Perhaps as significant as this question of self-fulfilling expectation in news judgment was the pattern of attention provided for the specific decisions. The birth control case was given top billing in the *New York Times* along with a related story on a bill introduced in the state legislature to liberalize New York's birth control law. The *Washington Post* and *Washington Evening Star* gave roughly equal coverage to both cases, although the *Post* favored slightly the birth control case and the *Star* gave somewhat greater attention to the *Estes* decision.

The AP and UPI both gave *Estes* considerably more coverage than *Griswold*, resulting in some interesting patterns of news display by the twelve papers randomly selected from a list of the 160 or so largest papers of morning-evening combinations.[42] The eight evening papers (June 7) involved were: *Houston Chronicle; Dallas Times Herald; Washington Daily News; Oklahoma City Times; Knoxville News-Sentinel; Long Beach* (Calif.) *Press Telegram; Spokane Chronicle;* and *Raleigh Times.* The four morning papers (June 8) were: *Detroit Free Press; Pittsburgh Post-Gazette; Nashville Tennessean;* and *Rochester* (N. Y.) *Democrat and Chronicle.*

As would be expected, the Houston and Dallas papers gave special attention to both the return of the astronauts and the *Estes* case. By contrast in Tennessee, the Nashville paper gave birth control the major play, but Knoxville gave it only one half inch in small type— by far the least amount of attention among any of the dozen studied.

Both the Rochester and Detroit papers, using partly *New York Times*

---

42. Circulation size of the papers selected randomly ranged from about 25,000 to about 525,000. The list used was from "U.S. Daily Newspapers of Large Circulation," *The World Almanac* (1965), p. 544. While not all-inclusive, this annual listing is an especially convenient and representative sample of large circulation papers or news combinations.

News Service copy, gave the birth control decision greater attention than *Estes*. These were the only other papers in the group of twelve to do so. Thus, it would appear that the *Times*'s emphasis on the birth control decision directly affected news coverage given by *Times* News Service subscribers.

Besides giving top attention to the *Estes* decision, the Pittsburgh paper, also as expected, gave the most complete coverage of all twelve papers to the United Mine Workers decision: 24-column-inches from its own Washington bureau staff.

The two smallest papers involved—Spokane and Raleigh—showed perhaps the most significant coverage patterns of all. Both used roundup stories from the wire services which attempted to jam all the Court decisions into one news item. As determined by the wire services' leads, both gave the major coverage to *Estes*. The Spokane paper carried a 19-inch story on the Court on page 2—the only one of the twelve papers not to carry at least one Court story on page 1. The Raleigh paper, by far the smallest in size of all twelve, also carried the smallest amount of total copy: one 12-column-inch story on page 1.

The situation with the smaller papers reflects the crucial time-space problem. Smaller papers simply tend to carry less news than larger papers and will tend to look for the roundup-type stories as a means of carrying as much news as possible.

It can be argued that the fairest way to look at news coverage is in terms of percentage of space, not total inches used. Under this system, many small papers might be carrying a greater proportion of Court news than large papers. But, while appealing and commonly used, such an analytical approach fails to get at the question of the "extent" of coverage. The amount of news disseminated is not measured by the percentage of news space devoted to the Court; it has to be measured by the total number of words. Sheer volume does not at all indicate the quality of coverage, but the conclusion is obvious that a large paper is *potentially* able to give more thorough coverage to the Court. The obvious inference is that the person in Spokane or Raleigh who is really interested in news about the Court would be better off with the *New York Times* than with a local paper.[43] It might also suggest (depending, of course, on what is done

43. West Coast readers, of course, actually did have a chance for a while to buy the *Times* "directly" through its short-lived Western Edition.

with the Court news) that he should buy a larger Seattle or Charlotte paper.

Another problem directly related to space was the great variation in the amount of Court wire copy used. In the overview, the extent of copy used ranged from about 10 per cent to 50 per cent of what the wire services had sent originally from Washington. For example, the Tuesday morning roundup story by UPI totaling about 55 column inches was often slashed to a fraction of its original size. The obvious conclusion here is that while the wire services are greatly influencing what words are being used in stories, the number of these words used depends most on the editing decisions at local news desks throughout the country.

It is, indeed, ironic that by stressing roundup stories so much the wire services seem to be indirectly encouraging much of their copy to get trimmed by members or clients. In addition, this roundup style has created a sometimes artificial news situation where one Court decision will usually get "top billing" around the country. This situation exists even though there may be no one major Court decision or there may be three or four decisions of roughly equal value. But, because many newspaper and station clients and members like roundup stories that can be easily cut from the bottom, the wire services have caught themselves in the not-always-rational news dilemma of having to "build up" one Court decision and "play down" the others. The same problem obviously exists in other news fields.

The lead of one UPI story reflects still another constant dilemma that the newsman may face: to "popularize" or not to "popularize"? If so, how much so? The following item was the rewritten lead from the UPI Washington bureau for Tuesday morning, June 8:

> WASHINGTON, June 8 (UPI)—Television in the court room had a bad rating from the Supreme Court today and just barely escaped being declared altogether unconstitutional.
>
> On a 5-4 ruling, the Court yesterday reversed the swindling conviction of Texas farm financier Billie Sol Estes because parts of his state trial were televised. . . .

Here is a news story which had swung into interpretation with the added effort at catchy wording. It could be argued that the result misfired as an overly simplified and inappropriately casual start to a serious story. And, at first glance, the story would seem to have thrown the reader off and to have been misleading about declaring a practice "altogether unconstitutional."

Yet, with closer analysis, there are positive factors in this approach. Although a bit unorthodox in phrasing, the lead does come fairly close to reality in interpretation—especially in saying that the Court really does not like TV in the courtroom. The story also indirectly introduces the idea of later possible review. Most importantly, it does stress the central television issue first and not Estes, who, as a celebrity, tended to distract attention from the real legal point of the decision.

Thus, here is still another illustration of the constant difficulty of achieving a delicate balance in news work—a happy mix between content and interest and between the what "really happened" and the "color of what really happened." There is nothing definitive that can tell the newsman for sure what would be the most effective way to communicate here. And yet he must constantly try to find out. He must unendingly juggle this delicate balance as he makes yet another trial-and-error effort to get a fact, idea, or concept across to an amorphous and diverse audience.

The analysis of typical Court coverage probably turns up no more revealing news judgment problems than those faced in headline writing. Here, heightened, are such basic news decisions as selection and emphasis of stories, space allotted, and interest, clarity, and perspective in phrasing.

By using the twelve randomly selected papers studied in the *Estes* decision in 1965 and adding the Dr. Sam Sheppard fair trial-free press case in 1966, the patterns become clear. Often the names of individuals in Supreme Court cases get greater attention in headlines than the legal issues.[44] In the 1965 case, ten of the twelve papers noted Estes specifically by name in headlines; four failed even to note the television-in-the-courtroom issue. With the 1966 case, eleven of the twelve mentioned Sheppard by name, and only three explicitly noted the fair trial issue before the Court.

The question here is not so much whether a newspaper should

44. For details on the headline coverage analysis here, see the author's "Supreme Court Headlines: Accuracy vs. Precision," *Columbia Journalism Review*, Summer, 1966, pp. 26–29.

carry such headlines as "High Court Upholds King's Conviction," [45] as what the possible effects of such stress seem to be. It obviously helps the readers for identification purposes to have Martin Luther King specified by name. But what happens, as with most Court decisions, when the legal issues are really more significant than the personality involved? One result would seem to be that perspective and understanding of the event are partially lost or, at minimum, de-emphasized. Both reporter at the Court and headline writer on the news desk face serious questions when the "big name" involved is allowed to interfere with or overpower the real news event—the legal issue.

A Summary Assessment

By analyzing types of coverage problems and representative 1965/67 decision days and cases, it is clear that many of the news-gathering and editing problems are not unique to Supreme Court coverage. The difference often seems to be that the problems are simply intensified by the complex task of interpreting both the multiple, detailed opinions of the justices and the silence of their Court orders.

Clearly, newsmen at the Court are most affected by the "whims" of the news day—the complex mix of exactly which cases the Court is deciding and how many. Despite efforts by newsmen to cover the Court carefully and consistently, the reporting of any one decision may be influenced by other decisions with which it must compete for attention.

Looking at patterns of coverage still another way shows other weaknesses on the part of the press—again, not just unique to the Court coverage situation but perhaps intensified by it. For example, except in the *New York Times, Washington Post,* and a very few other papers, there is little attention paid to the Court as an institution. Perhaps only a newspaper like the *Times* or a special column such as the weekly section on "law" in *Time* can ensure that the broader legal trends do not get lost in the shuffle of "spot news." Perhaps even more disturbing, especially in wire service coverage, is the failure to pull together the complicated pieces. Responsibility here rests with both the newsman at the Court and his superiors. Whoever is to

45. Example from the *Chicago Sun-Times,* June 13, 1967.

blame most, the long-term underlying "news" of the Court tends to be superficially treated and forced to take a second priority to coverage of major decisions as they are poured out by the justices.

One way to illustrate this basic weakness is to examine part of a story in the April 11, 1967, *Chicago Sun-Times* (p. 56):

SEABOARD-COAST MERGER GETS OK

WASHINGTON (UPI)—The Supreme Court ruled Monday that the merger of the Seaboard Air Line and the Atlantic Coast Line Railroads, in progress since 1958, may be completed.

Seaboard's head office is in Richmond, Va. Atlantic Coast Line is headquartered in Jacksonville, Fla. Tahe [sic] merged system, to be known as the Seaboard-Coast Line, will operate in Virginia, the Carolinas, Georgia, Florida and Alabama. It will control the Louisville & Nashville Railroad.

The Interstate Commerce Commission approved the consolidation in 1963.

In a brief order Monday, the court affirmed a decision of June 8, 1966, by a special three-judge federal court in Jacksonville, Fla., upholding the commission. . . .

Not until the fourth paragraph does the story note what really happened: the Supreme Court let stand a lower court ruling. Indeed, the most important fact was that the merger could now take place. But the impression, partly from the headline and partly from the lead paragraph, was that the Supreme Court had given approval. The story, though apparently factually correct, was misleading as to what exactly the Court does. The opportunity to show the Court's development of the law here was missed. How did this decision square with others? Did any significant legal principles evolve?

It may not be interesting or "catchy" to say that the Supreme Court "let stand a lower court ruling" rather than saying it "ruled"; but, unfortunately for the newsman, the wordier phrasing is closer to what actually happened from the standpoint of law.

From analysis of this story and other representative stories and headlines, it would seem that much of the press reporting problem could be expressed in terms of "imprecision" rather than "inaccuracy." [46] The semantic line between the two terms is, at best,

---

46. For further discussion and examples on this point, see, again: "Supreme Court Headlines: Accuracy vs. Precision," pp. 26–29. Also, in part: Wallace Carroll, "Essence, Not Angle," *Columbia Journalism Review*, Summer, 1965, pp. 4–6.

thin. Often the terms can be used interchangeably. But there are differences in connotation that carry considerable implications for coverage of such a complex and technical news field as the law. If accuracy can be defined roughly as "freedom from error" and precision as roughly "exactness or fineness of measurement," then the obvious question can be raised: Is it enough that a story be "accurate"—just free from error? What is the most satisfactory news goal: accuracy or the dimensions of "nearness to reality" and long-term perspective on the event?

Such concepts, while obviously overly demanding on any worker with words, would seem appropriate standards or goals for the press. By varying degrees, much of the press coverage of the Court seems to be falling short on these counts. Acknowledging all the problems and demands on the Court newsman, this analysis of typical coverage still indicates that the press is not providing enough perspective on the Supreme Court as the important governmental institution it really is. There is a general absence of penetrating coverage of long-term trends and legal developments, while much of the short-term news coverage that does exist ends up preoccupied with the drama of the "new event" or the persons and organizations involved and not enough with the why and the explanations of what it all *really means*, anyhow.

V

The Flow
of Information

DIFFUSION OF NEWS TO
SPECIAL INTEREST GROUPS AND AUDIENCES

MORE THAN JUST mass news media are involved in any process of information dissemination. Because so many factors can intervene between the newsman and his audience, it is essential to outline briefly some of the other elements in the communication of Court decisions. Also, in assessing the whole question of Court communication, it is important to look at some of the efforts considered or under way to change the situation.

Diffusion in General and Specifics

Important in any communication is the human variable—the persons who may serve to relay information or reinforce it. Different labels can be applied to such individuals but most often they involve the concepts of "personal influence" and "opinion leadership." [1] The extent of such influence is often not known; but, while the evi-

1. Especially relevant here and later in this section: Elihu Katz and Paul F. Lazarsfeld, *Personal Influence* (Glencoe, Ill.: Free Press, 1955); Joseph T. Klapper, *The Effects of Mass Communication* (Glencoe, Ill.: Free Press of Glencoe, 1960); and Bernard Berelson and Gary A. Steiner, *Human Behavior* (New York: Harcourt, Brace & World, 1964).

dence is not firm, it is clear that often news information follows the "two-step flow"—from the mass media to perhaps an opinion leader or person with an informational role and then on to others. To phrase the process another way: much of the news information received is indirect, often filtering down through personal contacts.

Complicating this process even further are the many other factors determining the content and extent of the communication message conveyed—for example, such concepts as reader and listener interest in and predisposition toward the news event.

In the overview, what such factors suggest is that a sheer increase in quantity of information about an institution such as the Supreme Court will not guarantee anything and especially not that the news message will be received or understood.

In the specific situation at the Court, a significant pattern evolves from the cycles of interest. During periods of controversy, as expected, the Court gets more public attention than during the periods of relative calm. And these cycles of interest tend to die off slowly. For example, extra copies of the June, 1962, New York Regents school prayer decision had to be printed until March, 1964, by the United States Government Printing Office. Staff around the Supreme Court Building also noticed that interest in the 1962 and 1963 prayer decisions among tourists did not decline noticeably until the fall of 1964.[2]

Such evidence quickly reinforces how much more than just the mass news media are involved in the spread of information about Court opinions. Besides the distribution of extra copies of individual decisions, the Government Printing Office also sells about 2,000 copies a term of its bound volumes of U.S. Reports while another 1,500 or so subscribers get preliminary prints of the Reports or the slip opinions (proofs) used by newsmen at the Court. Along with the two other major authoritative editions of Court opinions (Supreme Court Reporter and Lawyers Edition) and the commercial legal services (U.S. Law Week and that of the Commerce Clearing House),

2. Based on interviews and correspondence with Court and Government Printing Office staff, May and June, 1965. The GPO sold about 13,500 copies of the 1962 prayer decision—the largest public demand for any one opinion that anyone can remember. By contrast, about 9,300 copies of the 1963 prayer decision were sold—still a high figure but markedly below the more controversial 1962 case.

there are probably a total of 15,000 to 20,000 copies of full Court opinions circulating throughout the country.[3]

Although relatively limited in number, these full texts are obviously very important in the later stages of communicating Court decisions. In general, the mass news media are the earliest sources of information on Court action. Though the full texts are eventually distributed, the news media still remain as a primary resource to which most followers of the Court have been exposed. Still later come the many books and law review articles which add further embellishments. All of these become resources for the individual who may be in a crucial position to influence or convey information about the Court to others —his "peers, superiors, and inferiors."

The Flow to Public Officials

"I don't think Supreme Court decisions are read by 10 per cent of government officials. . . . Many rely on the *New York Times* and *The Washington Post*."

This estimate by a former Court newsman might be too conservative but the exact percentages are much less important than the general pattern. Throughout Washington (as elsewhere), law is left largely to the lawyers. In drafting legislation, it is the lawyers who are most often consulted; when questions about Supreme Court decisions arise, it is usually the staff counsels who are called in.

As noted earlier, the Solicitor General's Office probably follows the Court as closely as any public or private group in the country. But, otherwise, such governmental groups as Congress, the federal agencies, and other executive departments usually follow the Court only when a few cases of special interest arise.

There are many reasons for such inattention and apathy about most Court decisions. Most obviously, there is simply too much else to do other than to pay attention to a Court decision that may be only indirectly related to the governmental task at hand. And, too, Congressmen, as one example, are largely "mouth and ear men"—usually

3. Based on correspondence with New York lawyer, J. W. Riehm, June, 1965, and reinforced by Gilbert Cranberg, "What Did the Supreme Court Say?" *Saturday Review*, April 8, 1967, p. 90.

placing more importance on what they hear in personal interchanges than on what they read in the formal documents.[4]

The news media are often actively used by the public official for a digest of what is going on. As in the area of foreign affairs, there is evidence, indeed, that the press is used for Court news much more than many in the Washington establishment would like to admit. Although individuals differ markedly, governmental officials often read the *Times* and *Post* for Court news because these two papers are usually considered fairly reliable and complete in their coverage. (The circularity of cause-effect here has some intriguing implications: these papers continue to provide this type of coverage partly because they know they are being widely read by public officials because of this type of coverage.)

The importance of a Congressman's reliance on the news media is especially significant when such decisions as school prayer and reapportionment are considered. The Court's actions may bring an uproar on Capitol Hill—a reaction stemming partly from press interpretation of what the Court has said. For example, some Congressmen got early accounts of the 1962 New York Regents prayer decision through the wire service news tickers located in an alcove at the Capitol or from reporters asking for commentary about the decision. And, too, there were all the radio and televisions sets that helped convey such a big story. The result can be often a chain reaction of misunderstanding or confusion:

> No sooner has the Court performed the difficult task of interpreting the meaning of Congressional language . . . then one or more of Congress' several voices will be heard to damn the Court for having misconstrued the statute. . . . These are often isolated voices, but the press finds them newsworthy and it magnifies them. . . . Congressmen prefer condemning the Court in public orations to taking constructive effort to remedy what they consider to be the Court's errors.[5]

The evidence is also clear that many public officials (and private citizens) react negatively to the Court in this way without first trying

4. From especially: Bernard C. Cohen, *The Press and Foreign Policy* (Princeton, N.J.: Princeton University Press, 1963), pp. 208 and 217; and Donald R. Matthews, *U.S. Senators and Their World* (Chapel Hill, N.C.: University of North Carolina Press, 1960), p. 206.

5. Philip B. Kurland, "On Misunderstanding the Supreme Court," *Law School Record*, 9(1960): 31–32.

to find out exactly and fully what the Court has said.[6] (It is ironic that those who favor a Court decision may be just as uninformed but that usually the supporters of the Court do not say much and are not reported as much by the press. Praising a Court decision really is not very "exciting news." Such a position involves little conflict or controversy and, thus, news coverage of pro-court reaction tends to be used much less than anti-court.)

If one is concerned by the inattention of Congressmen and others to the Court and lack of solid information at early stages about what the Court has decided, what about the awareness of the Court on the part of the "most important" public official of all: the President? The question is especially intriguing.

In general, Presidents do not say much about Court decisions— in keeping with the concepts of "separation of powers" and the three supposedly distinct branches of government. The main exception in involvement would probably be Franklin Roosevelt with his Court-packing efforts during the 1930's. A more typical role would be found in former President Dwight Eisenhower's comment at a press conference when he pointed out that he was sworn to defend the Constitution and uphold the law. "Therefore, for me to weaken public opinion by discussion of separate cases, where I might agree or might disagree, seems to me to be completely unwise and not a good thing to do." [7]

It is especially interesting to note along this line that former President John F. Kennedy's reaction to the 1962 school prayer decision was much the same, though he placed more emphasis on advocating support of the Court's responsibility to interpret the Constitution. Also, while former President Harry S. Truman said much the same thing as Kennedy, Eisenhower and Herbert Hoover issued brief negative comments on the decision to the press.[8]

Indeed, one especially intriguing byproduct of all this is the ques-

6. Summary view based on interviews with Court and congressional staff personnel and newsmen (May–June, 1965) and on analysis of selected public statements. Reinforced especially by John H. Kessel, "Public Perceptions of the Supreme Court," *Midwest Journal of Political Science*, 10(1966): 167–91.

7. Quoted in Walter Murphy and C. Herman Pritchett, *Courts, Judges, and Politics* (New York: Random House, 1961), pp. 173–74.

8. From especially: William A. Hachten, "Journalism and the Prayer Decision," *Columbia Journalism Review*, Fall, 1962, p. 7.

tion of how the President himself finds out about Court decisions. One scholar has suggested that busy presidents probably have little time to read the actual Court opinions or full texts of justices' off-the-bench speeches.[9] Evidence collected on this question supports this view.

It is well established that President Kennedy used a combination of extensive consultation with advisers and reading of newspapers and magazines to obtain much of his information. Former staff members report that as far as they know he received nearly all of his information about the Court through newspapers.[10]

The pattern for President Lyndon B. Johnson is similar, if perhaps even more striking. Lee C. White, a former Special Counsel to the President, reported that there is no single way that Johnson stays informed but that:

> I would assume that the most usual means is through the wire service news tickers. The President follows them rather closely, and I would assume that they customarily provide him the first information he has about the Supreme Court decisions.
>
> If a particular decision requires an analysis or evaluation, it is the Justice Department that would be asked to provide it or would do so on its own initiative.[11]

Evidence is that even presidents cannot find out much in advance about what the Court is up to. No special arrangements to obtain special information about the Court are apparently provided; most of any limited "inside information" comes out only after the specific decision has been announced. Only in Court appointments does the President apparently have extra knowledge and extra power.

It might be argued that the President does not need to be especially well informed about the Court. But over-all evidence is to the con-

9. Walter F. Murphy, *Elements of Judicial Strategy* (Chicago: University of Chicago Press, 1964), p. 147.
10. Personal communication from Theodore Sorensen as relayed through his Washington staff in a June 22, 1965, personal letter, and reinforced partly by the many "Kennedy books" which have appeared since. (It is also interesting in this context that Sorensen has been quoted as saying: "In the White House I felt sorry for those who had to make judgments on the basis of daily newspapers." Quoted in A. H. Raskin, "What's Wrong with American Newspapers," *New York Times Magazine*, June 11, 1967, p. 28. The comment did not refer specifically to U.S. Presidents but by implication would seemingly have to, at times, include them.)
11. Personal letter, June 10, 1965.

trary, especially nowadays when there are so many areas of overlapping legislative-executive-judicial concern. The modern-day President has had to become an "all-knowing" leader, someone who (partly for political motivations) needs to be able to appear on a live television newscast and sound well informed on almost any question the press might toss his way. The President, like other elements in a democratic government, has to do his homework on the Court through his own reading and help from his staff. The mass news media are simply providing one of his primary textbooks.

The Flow to Other Interest Groups: Public and Private

Special interest groups can appear in the form of many organizations, such as farm, labor, business, religious, racial, military, law enforcement, or professional. There are so many groups of this type, in fact, that it is hard to trace exactly how patterns of news about the Supreme Court reach them. In general, however, communication about the Court filters down through channels similar to that for most public officials.

Attention may range from a casual following of the Court to an intense interest in a specific case or even an involvement in the litigation before the Court. To law enforcement agencies, for example, any cases dealing with the rights of criminals and suspects become of sustained concern. The groups involved may be quasi-public or entirely private.

Among the most interested groups today in following the Court are the police and related law-enforcement agencies. The recent Court decisions concerning confessions and the rights of accused to legal counsel have resulted in the distribution of considerable literature and information on the Court. As one example, the Chicago police department has distributed the complete text of the Court's opinion on interrogation in the *Escobedo* case as part of its training program.[12]

Not all such concern by semi-public or private interest groups, of

12. Chicago Police Department, *Law Training Bulletin Series*, Vol. 1, No. 2, Sept. 23, 1966.

course, is strictly informational. Much of the attention might be best described as the "professional struggle" to interpret what the Court has said mixed with complaints about the lack of guidelines provided by the Court. Police officials are often critical regarding the suspect's civil rights or on questions of obscenity. It is not surprising that many such groups are also among the quickest to criticize the Court for everything from corrupting American morals and protecting the criminal elements of society to just plain "bad laws" or bad opinion writing.[13]

There is nothing startling in the conclusion that much of the critical attention to the Court comes from those individuals and groups who are basically "result-oriented" and who do not like what the Court has been doing.[14] The lawyers and experts in law within such groups are usually given the task of disseminating information to members—through newsletters, public relations releases, speeches and articles, informal contact, and word of mouth. Here, again, the concepts of opinion leader and diffusion of information are important. Just as within the news media, there are "gatekeepers" who are crucial in determining the information and opinion disseminated about Court decisions and judicial appointments. Even with such a group as the American Bar Association, it is often only a small number of lawyers within it who are vocal and active in spreading news and opinion about Court legal trends.

To illustrate this system of informational flow even further, it is helpful to look at such "activist" groups as the National Association for the Advancement of Colored People, the American Jewish Congress, and the American Civil Liberties Union. These organizations have certain common interests in civil rights and action through liti-

13. Among the many examples, see: O. W. Wilson (former Chicago superintendent of police): "Crime, the Courts, and the Police," *Journal of Criminal Law, Criminology and Police Science,* 57(1966): 296; and Robert C. Finley (Justice, Supreme Court of the State of Washington), "Who is on Trial—The Police? The Courts? Or the Criminally Accused?" *Journal of Criminal Law, Criminology and Police Science,* 57(1966): 381–82.

14. From Anthony Lewis, "The Court and Its Critics," *Minnesota Law Review,* 45(1960–61): 308; Robert G. McCloskey, *The American Supreme Court* (Chicago: University of Chicago Press, 1960), p. 72; and Fred Rodell, "The 'Warren Court' Stands Its Ground," *New York Times Magazine,* Sept. 27, 1964, p. 120.

gation. In fact, all tend to stress lobbying through legal channels (i.e., taking issues into the courts).[15]

Thus, it is especially significant to find out that (while each works with extensive resources of legal documents) much of the information used by these groups comes from the news media.[16] Such information, especially initially, may be obtained from a news broadcast, a news ticker, or a newspaper, or from direct contact with a newsman who has called for comment or reaction on a specific Court case.

In all three organizations, interpretation of what the Court has said is left primarily to staff lawyers. Later, these interpretations may be used directly or indirectly in public comments by organization officials or as the basis for news releases and publications for members. In turn, some of this information is then diffused to other special interest groups and individuals and even back to the news media.

The special importance of this communication process can be seen during the day or so after a Court opinion has been announced. For most individuals or groups, full opinions of the Court are not available outside of Washington until the next morning at the earliest. Even those in Washington likely will have a delay of at least several hours in getting the full text; many may not see it until the next morning.

In the meantime, the press may be hard at work getting public reaction. And, as one civil rights official candidly commented: "Occasionally we wait until we have had an opportunity to read the entire decision before preparing our comment."

Occasionally? This means that usually reaction is based on incomplete data, with the role of the press again primary in the early flow of information and resulting opinion on what the Court has said.

EFFORTS TO IMPROVE THE FLOW

Besides some of the changes which have already been made at the Court (the elimination of Monday-only opinion days, for example), ef-

---

15. Fowler Harper and Edwin Etherington, "Lobbyists Before the Court," *University of Pennsylvania Law Review*, 101(1952–53): 1172; and Clement E. Vose, "Litigation as a Form of Pressure Group Activity," *The Annals*, 319(1958): 22–23.

16. Based on personal letters received from officials of the three groups, June, 1965.

forts are being made to solve problems in two other especially significant areas. The long-term significance and implications of these ventures dwarf many of the minor changes made or considered; they also have special relevance for other news fields.

The Lawyer and the Educator

The role, or potential role, of the organized bar in this communication situation is crucial when any attempt is made to assess total responsibilities for public understanding or misunderstanding of the Court. But while lawyers are probably the single most relevant special interest group that serves as a natural intermediary, the evidence is that "few members of the Bar are any more familiar with the work of the Supreme Court than are other semi-educated people in the community." [17]

As with government officials, many reasons exist why lawyers may be so inattentive to the Court. Many, for example, seldom get involved in the "Supreme Court types" of Constitutional issues; others, through the rise of corporations and government work, have had to specialize and narrow their legal interests. But it can also be said simply that the bar has often been too preoccupied with its own self-interests and has not cared enough to exert leadership in helping to improve understanding of the courts and administration of justice.[18]

There is evidence that bar officials are being more careful today in what they say about the Court; at least, they are not adding as much to the confusion.[19] Also, stemming from a variety of motives,

17. Kurland, "On Misunderstanding the Supreme Court," p. 13.

18. Among the many sources here: Justice William J. Brennan, Jr., address, "The Role of the Court—the Challenge of the Future," Edward Douglass White Lecture Series, Georgetown University Law Center, Washington, D.C., March 16, 1965; and Judge Irving R. Kaufman, address, "The Press, the Courts, and the Law Schools: Toward Justice and an Informed Public," Tulane Law Review Association, New Orleans, April 29, 1965.

19. Perhaps the classic "bad" example was 1962 American Bar Association President John C. Salterfield, who himself was criticized for blurting out: "If the use of that Regents prayer is unconstitutional . . . then words on this coin (In God We Trust) are also unconstitutional." (Quoted in the *Washington Post*, July 7, 1962.) This conclusion about greater silence is also based on interviews and the obviously more restrained role of the ABA since its period of heaviest Court criticism in the late 1950's. The ABA's public image was apparently hurt most when Chief Justice Warren resigned from the organization in 1959 in protest against attacks on the Court from bar leaders.

many small but cumulatively significant positive steps are being taken by lawyers and educators in an effort to improve education, especially at the high school level, in principles of the Constitution and the Bill of Rights.[20]

So far, the educational venture most directly relevant to the problem of communicating the Court has been the effort by the Association of American Law Schools to provide background memoranda on cases for use by the news media. (Closely linked to this development is another recent change. "However important popular books and mass media reporting on the Supreme Court may be for public understanding of the judicial process, scholarly writing on this subject exerts a deeper influence—on lawyers, on college and law-school training, and sometimes on the judges themselves." [21] While law professors have always been active in writing about the Court, much of the commentary had been confined to law reviews and scholarly books. But in recent years, noticeably more has appeared in the mass media, especially magazines.)

The AALS venture, started in the fall of 1964, was actually not new in its conception but was the first full-scale, sustained, direct assault to try to help the news media grasp the complexities of the Court.[22] The AALS effort grew out of a project of that organization's Committee on Education for Professional Responsibility in 1963, where a discussion evolved concerning attacks on the Supreme Court that were based on misunderstanding. The discussion eventually turned and centered on inadequacies of press coverage of the Court. The final outcome was creation of a panel of fifty to sixty advisers (law school professors) who agreed to be available to write up one or two background memoranda during each term of the Court. During the formation period in 1964, organizers met with newsmen to get their

20. Among the many possible examples, one of the most interesting has been the effort by the National Council of Social Studies, which in the fall of 1965, started distributing an insert called *Judgment* (in its regular magazine, *Social Education*) that outlines and explains major Court cases.

21. Alan F. Westin, "The Business of the Court," *New York Times Book Review*, March 7, 1965, p. 3.

22. Material in this section is based largely on interviews and correspondence with AALS committee members and the many other participants involved and on such Association documents as *Program and Reports of Committees*, 1963 annual meeting, and *Proceedings, Part I, Reports of Committees*, 1964 and 1966 annual meetings, and draft report for the 1966–67 program, September, 1967.

suggestions and conferred with Chief Justice Warren to get his approval and to arrange for copies of petitions for certiorari, briefs, and other supporting documents to be loaned out to the AALS.

The memoranda, now covering nearly all of the more than 150 Court calendar cases each term, are written up in factual and interpretative form by the expert assigned. Possible ways that decisions might be decided are noted, but predictions are avoided. Signs of partisanship are forbidden, although some editing of the analyses is needed on occasion to weed out expressions of opinion. (A copy of one AALS memorandum is included in Appendix C.)

Originally, the AALS project was designed primarily for the dozen or so most regular newsmen at the Court. But as the program began to take shape, it became apparent that there was a much wider audience for the memoranda. By the summer of 1965, without much publicity, more than one hundred newsmen were on the mailing list in Washington and around the country. Since then the number has increased steadily to more than two hundred.

Originally it was planned to have a law professor in the press room on decision days to post a marked-up copy of the memorandum for newsmen to use once a decision was handed down. This ambitious part of the project, however, soon ran into snags. It became evident that newsmen in their haste on decision days did not have much time to go back over the memoranda; the analyses, while helpful, did not help get the news copy out quickly. AALS panel members had also hoped to be able to answer newsmen's questions, but the evidence is clear that the Court staff, apparently including Chief Justice Warren, did not like this idea. While giving the general project encouragement and praise, the Chief Justice and Press Officer Bert Whittington gave no support to the presence of law professors in the press room. Because of a concern that such interpretation could be construed as coming from the Court, the Press Officer's view was simply that newsmen should be as free to do as they wanted outside the Court building or by phone but that it was improper to have law professors available for comment on the scene.[23]

In addition to these factors, the AALS group found their press room role on Mondays to be terribly time-consuming. With the change

23. Interview with Whittington, May 6, 1965.

in the Monday-decision-day policy, this part of the task became even harder. Eventually the press room part of the project was dropped.

Any evaluation of the AALS venture is difficult because of great problems in trying to establish cause and effect. In general, though, the evidence is that newsmen, especially editorial writers away from Washington, find the memoranda at minimum helpful and perhaps often "essential," providing valuable information not available elsewhere.[24]

It does seem ironic, then, that the project has had to struggle for recognition among newsmen (and some lawyers) and has had trouble in switching over from a no-fee to a fee basis. Newsmen and news executives seem to like the service but are just not very excited about having to pay for it.[25]

The memoranda have not been without other problems—coming too late, for example (on occasion even after the decision has been announced). But despite these early difficulties and controversies and some that remain, the program must still rate as one of the most significant large-scale voluntary projects ever attempted by any profession to help the news media with a communication problem. The effort involved in the preparation of each memorandum has been considerable, and the reward to the writer has been little (and nothing monetarily).

Interestingly, the project also has had a fringe benefit of perhaps considerable significance: it has created an atmosphere of better understanding and awareness of problems between newsmen and legal scholars. As one panel member wrote, after receiving a note of praise from the AALS office for a memorandum well-done: "Actually, I

24. Based, again, on interviews and correspondence with newsmen and other participants and reinforced by Cranberg, "What Did the Supreme Court Say?" See also: letter to the communications editor, *Saturday Review*, May 13, 1967, p. 82, by Professor Jerome A. Barron, 1966–67 chairman of the AALS Supreme Court Decisions Committee, and report of the Committee, 1966 annual meeting of the AALS.

25. For published testimony on the financing problem, see Professor Barron's letter to *Saturday Review*, May 13, 1967, p. 82. The project also had early trouble getting publicity into the trade magazine, *Editor & Publisher*, and other news media sources. For examples of vocal critics of the project, see especially columnist Arthur John Keeffe in the *American Bar Association Journal*, March, 1965, p. 287, and May, 1965, p. 501.

found it very difficult to do. Henceforth I shall have more respect for the popularizers."

Training the Newsman

It would be too easy to look at the Supreme Court news coverage and say that many of the problems could be solved by merely adding more experienced personnel. Certainly quantity is important; but just as obviously, much of the question centers on the elusive dimension of "quality."

It is not at all surprising that several news executives, when asked about Court coverage, said they wished they could find a newsman as competent as Anthony Lewis to cover the Court. Not only is it hard to get such a skilled person for such a news job, it is also hard to keep him. With the lure of advancement, it may well be inevitable that a top-level specialist would eventually want to leave his assignment and seek new worlds to conquer.[26] In partial contrast with specialization in the academic world, not only is there the danger of going stale with a news specialty by becoming "too expert," there are often the positive lures of a bureau chief assignment or other high-paying, more influential positions of news management. Or, perhaps there is the attraction of more money and more challenge in a field other than news work.

But despite such drawbacks, several news organizations have been able to attract a new breed of journalist to the Court beat. Many of these now have either law degrees or at least some special training in law. The indications are that, indeed, many of these have been doing "well" in their coverage.[27]

26. View expressed by several of the newsmen interviewed, especially James Reston, May 26, 1965.

27. Among the "regular" former or current Court reporters with law degrees are Fred Graham of the *New York Times*, Dana Bullen of the *Washington Evening Star*, and Jack C. Landau of Newhouse National News Service. Those with an academic year of training at Harvard Law School include the two "pioneers," Anthony Lewis of the *Times* and James Clayton of the *Washington Post*, and John P. MacKenzie of the *Post*. (It is interesting that lawyers Bullen and Landau have also taken a year off to study constitutional law at Harvard under Nieman Fellowships.) Data in this section is based partly on interviews, May and June, 1965, with all of these newsmen—except Lewis who had to be communicated with by mail from his then-new assignment as London bureau chief for the *Times*.

Whether such a new wave of law-trained Court newsmen is a positive and significant development is not as simple a question, however, as some might suppose. As might be expected, those who have the training usually strongly favor it and those that do not tend to regard it lightly. The basic argument of those opposed to legal training is that a year's on-the-job experience tends to be more valuable than a year of studying law.[28]

Those who favor the legal training tend to agree with Lewis that: "A bad reporter would not be made a good Supreme Court correspondent by a year at law school. . . . A good reporter with an interest in the field will be made much, much better able to do the job by at least a year of legal training focused on the Supreme Court." [29] Such advocates also argue the importance of plain old self-confidence: a reporter with legal training is able to face just about any story with a feeling for the law, and he can judge the really important aspects of a case. Such confidence also may help a newsman with his sources; it certainly does not hurt a reporter at all (as a foot in the door with lawyers and judges) to be able to say he has studied a year of law at Harvard. Here, indeed, is one way for the reporter to accelerate his reputation as informed and "trustworthy." Part of his reputation may be positively affected by his image of legal training, but often the training itself has provided real background knowledge that enables greater understanding of the legal issues with news sources.

There are a variety of arguments raised against such training that could be relevant in any assessment, such as: the danger of writing too much for lawyers; becoming too favorable toward the institution of the Supreme Court; or becoming too restless with some of the routine and pressures of day-to-day legal news coverage.[30]

For some impressionary but worthwhile evidence of the possible success by this "new breed" of Court newsman, it is perhaps most relevant to note the American Bar Association's 1967 special awards for coverage to MacKenzie and also to Landau and Adam Clymer of the *Baltimore Sun* and *Time* magazine (reported in *Editor & Publisher*, July 8, 1967, p. 12).

28. Among those who hold this view is Press Officer Whittington, a former United Press newsman at the Court (interviewed May 6, 1965).

29. Letter from Lewis, May 18, 1965.

30. These were among the criticisms sometimes pointed at the *Times's* Lewis. Although analysis of his writing indicates Lewis' coverage did tend at times to fall into these traps, he was, in general, able to control such tendencies so that his coverage over-all would be rated even by most of his critics as usually well written, clear, informed, and "not too biased."

But on balance, even such criticism of legal training is not so much centered on the philosophy as on the practice and on questions about what the best ways are to provide this background. Should papers seek lawyers and try to turn them into journalists or hire journalists who can learn the law? And what kinds of legal training are going to best help the Supreme Court newsman?

Such are the types of questions faced by the lawyers, newsmen, and educators. For the news media, much of the puzzle seems to go back to a long-standing pride in "the generalist"—the reporter who is supposedly able to cover a variety of stories without special expertise or even any prior knowledge of a subject. But again, even those who defend this concept of a journalistic "jack-of-all-trades" do not tend to dispute the view that today's newsman must be better educated and trained. The debate seemingly centers most over exact definitions of "better education" and "training" and whether the costs are worth the effort.

Perhaps in this whole dialogue an element of compromise is needed, based on what the press really is and could be. The nature and role of the mass news media are such that the journalist must be careful to avoid being either too idealistic or too practical. And he should also avoid setting his sights at too low a professional level. For the specializing newsman, in any field, there may be, indeed, a half-truth in the barbed view that he needs to avoid the extremes of being either the expert who knows more and more about less and less until he knows everything about nothing, or the generalist who knows less and less about more and more until he knows nothing about everything.[31]

31. William L. Laurence, "Science in the News," in George L. Bird and Frederic E. Merwin (eds.), *The Press and Society* (New York: Prentice-Hall, 1951,) p. 314.

VI
The Overview

THERE IS A DANGER in trying to explain everything in terms of communications problems or in overestimating the significance of modern-day communication difficulties.[1] Thus, this analysis of Supreme Court communication problems should be considered as only one way to approach many of the issues raised here; it is, hopefully, however, one of the most productive routes:

> Accurate and adequate communication between groups and people will not in itself bring about the millennium, but it is a necessary condition of almost all forms of social progress. Physical barriers to communication are rapidly disappearing, but the psychological obstacles remain. These psychological difficulties are in part a function of the very nature of the language; in part, they are due to the emotional character and mental limitations of human beings.[2]

As this study has shown, there are still "physical problems" in the communication of Supreme Court decisions. But clearly, many of these physical dimensions (such as time and space) are self-imposed —determined by the institutions of the Court or by the news media.

1. Earl Johnson, former UPI vice-president, "Symposium: Trends Ahead in Public Affairs Reporting," *Journalism Quarterly*, 40(1963): 443. Also: Harold Lasswell, *The Future of Political Science* (New York: Atherton Press, 1963), pp. 233–34.
2. Daniel Katz, "Psychological Barriers to Communication," in Wilbur Schramm (ed.), *Mass Communications* (Urbana: University of Illinois Press, 1960), p. 316.

While the pressures on all participants are often great and complex, this would seem to be a situation in which many of the barriers to effective communication can be identified, assessed, and perhaps broken down.

It is also essential to stress that such breakdowns in an idealized perfect flow of ideas are not merely problems for the law. Scientists, educators, businessmen, religious leaders, and others are among the many specialists disturbed by mass media coverage.[3] The law is not alone—either in having the news coverage problem or in having difficulty within its profession in doing much about the problem.

In trying to assess responsibilities here it is important to acknowledge the seemingly fundamental conflict in roles between press and government. As one connector between the governors and the governed, the press indeed gets caught in the middle. Quite literally, it is often damned if it does and damned if it doesn't. A basic reason for this role conflict is that the lawyer (or judge) and journalist have not only different goals but also different techniques. The issue before the Supreme Court is painstakingly laid out in specific and technical language; the newsman, by contrast, is trying to hurry a "translation" of the specific into the general for his mostly non-law-trained and often already-biased readers or listeners.

The result is that news coverage, while in many ways having improved in recent years, is often inadequate or not nearly as helpful as it could be for the person trying to understand and evaluate law in a democratic society. Whether the news media like the role or not, they are "educators"—burdened with responsibilities as conveyors of information and understanding of the day-to-day operation of government and society.[4]

It is, thus, disturbing in this situation when one editorial writer has to admit: "I have gotten so distrustful of Supreme Court coverage that we subscribe to *Law Week* and run no editorials on court opinions until we have the text."

3. J. Edward Gerald, *The Social Responsibility of the Press* (Minneapolis: University of Minnesota Press, 1963), pp. 108–9.

4. Among sources of the "educator" concept: Bernard C. Cohen, *The Press and Foreign Policy* (Princeton, N.J.: Princeton University Press, 1963), p. 24; and W. H. Ferry and Harry S. Ashmore, *Mass Communications* (Santa Barbara, Calif.: Center for the Study of Democratic Institutions, 1966), pp. 10–11.

It would be easy to rationalize away many of the difficulties by say-ing that law is complex and subjective and that everybody, thus, has a tough communications assignment. But while partly true, such an approach does not accomplish much in problem-solving nor in meeting the challenge of man's greater self-understanding and ration-ality.

Briefly, then, these final pages attempt to reach some conclusions about the communication forces at work and to offer some specula-tions and suggestions as to what might have been learned and what might be done. The starting point here is the Supreme Court, be-cause the structure and means of information dissemination greatly affect what is transmitted to the news media and ultimately to the reading or listening consumer.

What the Court and Bar Might Do

In praising the Association of American Law Schools project which prepares beckground memoranda for use by the press, United States Appellate Judge Irving R. Kaufman was quick to stress the fol-lowing: "The really difficult problem, however, still remains—how to assist hard-pressed news reporters who must explain difficult opinions to the lay public under the pressure of looming deadlines." [5]

It does seem ironic that potentially the most important part of the AALS effort—the on-the-scene interpretation of Court decisions in the press room—was dropped. Interpretation of decisions "is the most important single thing you could undertake. Anybody can read a decision and find out what facts are involved and what the Jus-tices said. The difficult part is figuring out what they meant, and what it means for the future." [6]

Some of this communication problem exists because the Supreme Court is reluctant to do much about it. There are good reasons to resist change, but it would seem that the Court should be encourag-ing more informed dialogue about its activities rather than mostly

5. Address, "The Press, the Courts, and the Law Schools: Toward Justice and an Informed Public," Tulane Law Review Association, New Orleans, April 29, 1965.

6. Letter from James E. Clayton to Professor Henry Manne of the AALS, April 23, 1964.

just wishing for such dialogue. In fact, it seems somewhat inconsistent for the Court to talk about such First Amendment rights as freedom of the press as an essential part of democratic dialogue and yet discourage efforts at improved public insights into the Court itself and the workings of law. The Court often talks about the need for change in society and yet resists change in many of its own traditions and practices.

Perhaps the Court itself has been as guilty as any bar group of wanting to "leave law to the lawyers." The point here is not to urge any impropriety of disclosure or to violate the seemingly correct view that written Court opinions should "speak for themselves." There is no need to go beyond the words of the opinions; this view simply says that the Court should pay more attention to the problems of legal meaning for those not in the inner circle of awareness and sophistication.

"Perhaps the public image of justice is distorted because we judges have turned our backs to the news media." [7] Only partial understandings of courts and the law have been allowed to sift through the cloaks of secrecy and judicial language. All this has been true despite the belief that the citizen is entitled to know what judges are doing.[8]

Again, such an assessment does not argue for public disclosure of sensitive deliberations in the conference room or elsewhere; it does simply acknowledge that—like it or not—a Supreme Court decision is not just something that goes into a bound volume for lawyers and other judges. It is a declaration of governmental policy that (partly by definition of the role of the press in a democratic society) also becomes a public "news" event. As an important institution, it would seem that the Court should not only show more empathy with the real problems of the press and public understanding but also should consider even more seriously the full ranges of real, possible, positive steps that could be taken.[9]

7. Judge J. Skelly Wright, U.S. Courts of Appeals, "A Judge's View: The News Media and Criminal Justice," *American Bar Association Journal*, December, 1964, p. 1129.

8. Judge Jerome Frank, *Courts on Trial* (Princeton, N.J.: Princeton University Press, 1949), pp. 2–3.

9. The concept of empathy here is drawn especially from Robert Cooley Angell, *Free Society & Moral Crisis* (Ann Arbor: University of Michigan Press, 1958), p. 211.

While well within its rights to expect that criticism will be informed and that other groups should work to improve the communication problem, the Court can also move positively on its own. As a starter, it might help to acknowledge that:

> To command public confidence and respect, judicial authority need not be transcendent, awe-inspiring, immune to criticism—screened from the public eye. The Court's firm command over the hearts and minds of men is not grounded in mystery, but in the contemplative pause and the sober second thought its restraining power entails.[10]

Why is there the cloak of confusion and uncertainty rather than clarity? The Court should assess this question carefully, perhaps most logically by starting with its written opinions that become the law.

Justices can be even more aware about the problems of vague wording and "legal language." In particular, any potential confusing elements should be watched carefully; wherever possible, the Court should be candid in outlining exactly what it has and has not decided. It should be careful to distinguish between what is law and what are *obiter dicta*—incidental remarks that sometimes confuse what the Court has said.

It would seem that clarity and care in judicial phrase-making are minimum standards of "good" law-making.[11] Wherever possible, the Court should try to *explain* its reasoning. Although more explanations of reasons for granting or denying writs of certiorari may not be "legally desirable" they do seem to be "societally needed."

While more multiple concurring and dissenting opinions would seem definitely undesirable, perhaps at times the justices might employ more clarifying opinions that could help both legal expert and layman to figure out exactly what has been said. (For one such example, see Appendix D and the concurring opinion of Justice William J. Brennan, Jr., which helped give perspective in the complex *Estes* v. *Texas* decision.)

The Court should also help to speed more copies of its opinions to interested segments of society. Such increased dissemination and availability (including more copies of bound volumes for public—not

10. Alpheus T. Mason, "Myth and Reality in Supreme Court Decisions," *Virginia Law Review*, 48(1962): 1406.

11. Reinforced especially by Robert A. Leflar, "Some Observations Concerning Judicial Opinions," *Columbia Law Review*, 61(1961): 820.

just law—libraries) would not be merely a promotional practice. For the law to be understood, it needs to be accessible. Because the costs involved here would be small by comparison with the potential gains, the Court should encourage better means for public official and private citizen to obtain or have access to copies of decisions and have them as soon as possible—in hours and days, or in a week or two, rather than in weeks and months. This seems to be needed especially when major or controversial cases are involved.

Clearly much of this burden of obtaining Court decisions rests with the "consumer." It is here where the various bar groups and individual lawyers should help by encouraging and even demanding an informed, less-emotional dialogue on the law. All efforts at improved education and flow of rational information about the law should be encouraged and carried out by those closest to and most concerned about the legal system in a democracy.

There are specific changes that the Court also might consider in either the near or distant future. Separately, none of these may be important; but, collectively, they could go a long way in helping much of this communication problem, especially the difficulties most affecting the mass news media.

The Court has considered the idea of having a skilled interpreter of its decisions—someone who could help the newsmen understand the main legal issues involved. But the justices obviously have hesitated to take such a step. Although there are drawbacks, the idea should be given serious attention and perhaps tried. What is needed is an "expert" of some kind—not the traditional press agent—but someone who could help newsmen and lay publics by providing objective and non-promotional information about the legal issues.

Another change also considered and worthy of serious consideration is the possibility of having each case decision headnote (the very brief digest of a case) written up and released when the case is announced rather than afterwards. At present, headnotes are handled by the Court's staff reporter, who is the editor and publisher of the official *U.S. Reports*. After the opinion is handed down, he writes up the headnote and sends it to the majority opinion writer for approval. This summary has been used primarily as a quick guide for the legal researcher needing to skim through many decisions.

The headnote has not been prepared for use by the press but there seems to be little reason why the practice could not serve a dual purpose. Since headnotes have to be written anyway, why not hand them out along with the opinions rather than days or weeks later? No extra problems of secrecy are involved and, at most, the announcing of an opinion would be delayed only a day or two.[12] If well warned, the press could quickly learn to treat these for exactly what they are—helpful summary guidelines and *not* the decision of law handed down. Whatever the value of such a proposal, it does seem better than any kind of separate formal press releases that would try to "announce" what the Court has decided.

Still another logical alternative would be to make sure all opinions had a summary statement written into them—designed deliberately not only for the press but also for hard-pressed legal scholars and students. Some of the justices already tend to do this but the practice is too informal and inconsistent.

A more controversial proposal is for distribution of decisions to the press on a hold-for-release basis, with perhaps a "lock-up" arrangement whereby newsmen would be isolated from any contact with the outside world. Such a lock-up could be for a few minutes or for an hour or two. In either extreme the extra time available would enable more thoughtful handling of cases and might make it unnecessary for the wire services to rely on writing so much of stories in advance.

The lock-up idea, although not without problems, has merit, and it seems unfortunate that the Court has apparently already closed its mind to this possibility.[13] The main concern with secrecy is valid, but such a preoccupation would seem overdrawn because there have been apparently no violations of secrecy since at least the early 1900's. Security precautions at the Court are elaborate—with the tightly controlled flow of intra-Court communication helped most by the well-guarded print shop in the basement of the Court Building.

The argument that a justice should be able to change his mind up until the last moment has some value but not enough. Lock-ups would

12. Telephone interview with Court Reporter Henry Putzel, Jr., June 16, 1965. Putzel should not be considered as necessarily advocating such change; he simply said there was no reason why the headnotes could not be written in advance of announcement.

13. From Gilbert Cranberg, "The Court and Its Public: Warren's View," *Des Moines Register*, Oct. 16, 1966.

merely move up by minutes the time in which a decision would be released. Even then, there would be no advance public exposure; if necessary, the Court could demand that the press agree not to use any decision that suddenly had to be delayed.

The practice of advance release is so common in other government work (with just as many sensitive or economic issues at stake) that one can only wonder why the Court is so tradition-bound on this point. The law is special, but is it *so special* that possible logical alternatives to news dissemination should be so quickly dismissed? (Indeed, along this same line, is the Court *so special* that it could not be covered on occasion "live" or on tape by television? Again it would seem that the Court has been premature in apparently closing its mind to this possibility.[14] With either the oral arguments or the oral announcement of opinions on decision days, there is no fair trial-free press problem. Difficulties in maintaining the "dignity of the Court" do exist, but these seemingly could be well handled.[15] The potential for expanded public insight and understanding into the Court here is great and could certainly far outweigh most of the counter-arguments usually expressed.)

Still another major suggestion has already been adopted, in part, by the Court: the spreading out of decision days rather than letting them pile up. While abandoning Monday-only decision days has been helpful and necessary, it would seem that the Court could go even further. Not enough of the flood has been slowed—in fact, many times decision days still end up with too many cases. The last day of each term remains especially troublesome—as in 1967, when the Supreme Court reverted to its old practices and thirteen decisions were announced in only a few hours. Even three or four major cases on one decision day seem plenty for press and public to try to consume.

Each decision should be released as soon as possible on any day of the week, thus avoiding some of the problem of cases competing

14. Report of Chief Justice Warren's rejection of a formal request by the Columbia Broadcasting System for courtroom coverage of oral arguments can be found in the *New York Times,* June 14, 1965.

15. One of the easiest ways to control such a program might be to tape it and to allow time for editing and a careful commentary from newsmen and possibly guest legal experts. (Such a program also could be reproduced and distributed for use in schools, universities, and even law schools.)

against each other for news space. If necessary, the Court should declare regularly which will be the opinion-announcing days. Again, if needed, the justices could withdraw an opinion from the list for public release without having to give any explanation. With a little bit of planning and more concern for the press and the public it represents (and for its own self-good), the Court could easily help the informational flow without affecting the sanctity and proper procedures of both the Court and the law.

WHAT THE PRESS MIGHT DO

In the total view, it is encouraging that some news organizations have already made concrete efforts to improve coverage of the Supreme Court. But in light of their relatively important role in this communications situation, it would seem that the press over-all should have taken more leadership and initiative. It certainly can consider further steps in the future—not only in this area of legal coverage but also in many other evolving technical fields, such as science, medicine, education, or the social sciences.

In particular, the press needs to go after more of the long-term, sometimes philosophical, questions which exist. For example, news executives and editors must reassess policies about the types of news that are now being covered and those that should be offered. Can the Supreme Court be covered well by anything less than a full-time man? Should the Court be covered much like other news events, sometimes by reporters with little or no background in the complexity of law? Despite the obvious basic importance of the reporter on the scene, it still is crucial to acknowledge that he is only part of a total news organization. Administrative policies may hinder or help significantly the day-to-day coverage provided by those working in the field.

Such perspective does not free the Supreme Court reporter of responsibility, but it does acknowledge how management resources and awareness may greatly influence his working environment.

Newsmen at all levels need to be more aware and understanding of criticism being leveled at them—whether such criticism is fair or not. In particular, the news media must stop being overly defensive—often crying out against such criticism in the name of freedom of the press.

This super-sensitivity on the part of the media may be easing some-what; but still, while apparently aware of many of its own deficiencies, the press over-all does not like to be told by others what to do. At the same time, it fails to do much soul-searching on its own.

> As an institution, the press is big, fat, happy, and satisfied. It no longer digs for news but takes publicity handouts and passes them off as its own work. At a time when the society is changing from top to bottom, the press is not helping the people understand what is hap-pening.[16]

Whether one need is for "external" local or national press councils of private citizens (who would give regular critiques of press per-formance) or some sort of "internal" system for criticism within the industry does not seem as important as the basic need for "some-thing." Probably both systems of external and internal evaluation would be desirable, but such approaches still will only help if newsmen and media executives exhibit a genuine willingness to be evaluated and to be totally candid in any assessments. Evidence is that certain media leaders are already doing this or are willing to participate in such ventures; but, on balance, too many still seem indifferent and hos-tile to the idea or unwilling to give it more than token lip service.

Much less philosophically, there are other efforts that might be made to improve the total communication problem at the Court. The news media should reassess carefully their role as an interim source of information. "The press should not be a mere transmission belt for the reckless." [17] If it seeks to give reactions to Court decisions, it should take several specific steps. The press and its sources should be asked: "Have you (I) read the opinion?" Or, "How do you (I) defend that statement in light of the Court's ruling?" In turn, news sources should not hesitate to pressure newsmen for information they feel is necessary for a reasonable comment. Wherever possible, re-porters should have copies of the opinion or lengthy excerpts which

16. Gerald, *The Social Responsibility of the Press*, p. 109. Also on this general theme: A. H. Raskin, "What's Wrong with American Newspapers?" *New York Times Magazine*, June 11, 1967, pp. 28–29 and 77–84; "What's Wrong with the Press?" *Newsweek*, Nov. 29, 1965, pp. 55–60; and Andre Fontaine, "The Mass Media—A Need for Greatness," *The Annals*, 371(May, 1967): 72–84.

17. William Hachten, "Journalism and the Prayer Decision," *Columbia Journal-ism Review*, Fall, 1962, p. 8.

they could use and show to sources (or, at minimum, read to them by telephone).

And there is no reason why a news story could not give its readers extra insight through such phrases as, "While admitting he had not read the Court's decision, the Senator said. . . ."

Closely related to their important role in the early flow of Court information, the media (and wire services in particular) could do more to help harried and uninformed local editors. Both AP and UPI do such advising, but even more is needed. For example, to cut down preoccupation with speed and concern about what the competition is doing, one wire service might simply note: "We have a major Supreme Court civil rights story—with interpretation—coming in 20–30 minutes." In the 1962 prayer decision, for example, a special note might have helped: "Please note that only state-supported prayer was banned. Decision is narrow but has obvious long-term implications. Exact significance, though, unclear at this moment. Will try to clarify."

Such dialogues would cut down the amount of "news" that could be carried. But what is "news"? Is it just the end product of written words, or does it include the whole series of informational interchanges? Local news editors and headline writers especially need guidance from "expert reporters" on Supreme Court matters; and it would seem that valuable news ticker time could be better used for such an interchange of memos than for some of the columns, features, and other items often sent.

On this same theme of news transmission, it is important that early public commentary on Court decisions should be kept to a minimum. More often than not, 250 words of insightful interpretation on the decision are more valuable than 250 words of roundup reaction from often uninformed or already very pro- or anti-Court sources.

The whole need for greater emphasis on interpreting the Court as an institution (again, especially by the news wire services) is one telling argument for at least some legal training by any journalist trying to cover the Court. There are many other ways that legal expertise can be obtained, but none really seems to be a substitute for the potential insight, awareness, and perspective acquired by the reporter with a background in law. Again, the type of training seems less important here than the simple fact that some training should help.

There are other ways, too, in which the media could seek more outside help. In addition to utilizing the Association of American Law Schools memoranda to their fullest and giving the project needed financial backing, the press should take advantage of all the other resources that can be tapped. For example, as suggested by Chief Justice Earl Warren, the media might use "law clerks" to help on decision days or perhaps hire other non-government specialists to act as consultants.[18] The news media should have a full reservoir of legal experts who might be willing to be interviewed for interpretative features or news analyses and editorials on Court decisions or who might be willing to write (mostly for pay) articles or columns on Court decisions.[19]

Such "legal aid" will not help the press much in dealing with the problem of the flood of information. But at least such steps could improve the quality of coverage. The press must put more time, energy, and money into becoming more informed. Sometimes such effort can come indirectly at the local level by the demand of a news executive that another syndicated news service be purchased in addition to the AP and UPI coverage. Or perhaps the day will come when enough editors will be willing to invest in top-level AP and UPI coverage by demanding more and better personnel and less preoccupation with rushing mostly "spot news."

There are also ways for the press to better help the consumer handle a deluge of information. For example, the busy reader (especially of the Sunday *New York Times*) needs help in finding what has happened. Better and more indexing, cross-referencing, and greater care in headlines and news display, could all be helpful to the interested reader who has to struggle to find what he wants and *needs*.

Major analytical stories could also be repeated. What would prevent some large newspapers, for example, from carrying a monthly or

18. The Chief Justice' suggestion has been noted by Gilbert Cranberg, "'What Did the Supreme Court Say?" *Saturday Review*, April 8, 1967, p. 92. *Time* magazine's approach of using a part-time legal consultant for its "Law" section is seemingly an excellent way to try to give greater accuracy and perspective in coverage. Such use of experts, however, can be expensive.

19. One especially interesting approach has been that of the District of Columbia Medical Society, which periodically distributes a list of doctors and their specialties to area mass media with the understanding that, if possible, these specialists will help the press interpret medical questions and clarify complex technical matters.

an occasional extra edition of timely analytical and in-depth pieces? Instead of being considered "good for only one day," the daily newspaper (like its television counterparts and more enduring magazine competitors) could resort at times to rerunning important analytical stories or series.

Such "redundancy" (repetition) in coverage could help significantly to transmit understanding and ease some of the deadline pressures. For instance, one of the best times to cover a Supreme Court case is at the oral argument stage. Here is a chance for the press to lay out the issues and help, in part, to avoid much of the later shock or suddenness of the Court's action. At least a segment of the audience could have an insight into a case or an awareness of it long before it was finally announced in the courtroom. In addition (and perhaps as the most obvious fringe benefit), the newsmen freed to listen to and cover the oral argument would be likely to be much better equipped to cover the actual final decision. Many oral arguments already are covered but not often enough, not consistently enough, and not thoroughly enough.

In attempting to pull these ideas together more meaningfully, it is possible to summarize much of this Court news communication problem through what might be called a "hierarchy of news information conveyed":

1) Highest Level: Understanding and Meaning
2) Middle Level: Ideas, Facts and Details
3) Lowest Level: Familiarity and Acquaintance

Each news story has potential levels of information which have both short-term and long-term significance. The newsman is faced with two overlapping but not identical communication problems: (1) Does this news story give understanding and meaning of the specific event described? (2) Does this news story give understanding and meaning of the general happening or trend of which this specific event is a part?

Although the newsman can never succeed completely in either situation, he can always try to succeed. Here is where the demands of "precision" rather than just "accuracy" are so vital in working toward this goal. To say that a story is "accurate" or "free from error" does not help the reporter much in achieving that top-level objective of reader perspective and "real grasp" of the issues.

In this total analysis, the problem of Court press coverage seems to mesh with the more general concern that the press is "not getting better fast enough." [20] The education of readers and listeners is improving and so are their needs in an ever more complex democratic society. Yet too many of the news media have seemingly not kept pace with the changes around them.

One reason for this disturbing situation is that the news media have operated too long on habit and tradition, hunch and intuition. But the proverbial seat-of-the-pants and off-the-top-of-the-head methods are seldom valid or seldom even satisfactory. In fact, the evidence is that often they do not work very well at all.

The news media have not been able to master many of their problems in the complex world of human communication. Messages are sent out but often only parts of them are received, let alone fully comprehended and retained. The press must acknowledge that much of its news gathering and news editing is, at best, only semi-systematic —that established news "formulas" for covering the police beat do not necessarily apply well in covering a complex court of law. All institutions in modern society, including the Supreme Court and the mass news media, are surrounded by change and are themselves changing. It is now time for the press to admit that it needs to be a little less the Art and to become a little more the Science.

20. Raskin, "What's Wrong with American Newspapers?" p. 77.

Appendix A
Methodology

"No man knows fully what has shaped his own thinking." This view, as expressed by Robert K. Merton in *Social Theory and Social Structure*, reflects much of the problem here. But in addition to the Bibliographic Note, a few other efforts at methodological highlights should be attempted.

MAIN CONCEPTS USED

Besides the obviously important concepts of the "strategic points of transmission," decision-making, and the "two-step flow of communications," there are several other themes that have been basic to this analysis. Two of these merit brief but special attention:

The "phenomenistic approach," drawn mainly from Klapper's *The Effects of Mass Communication*, says simply that the mass media are influential forces, not sufficient by themselves, working amid other forces. (This well-documented view helped push this analysis into looking at the total communications setting—rather than seeing the news media's coverage of the Court in an isolated cause-effect type of relationship.)

The Mathematical Theory of Communication of Shannon and Weaver focuses on such meaningful analytical themes as the "capacity of the communications channel" to convey a message. Ques-

151

tions such as the following are raised: "How accurately can the symbols of communication be transmitted?" (the technical problem) "How precisely do the transmitted symbols convey the desired meaning?" (the semantic problem) "How effectively does the received meaning affect conduct in a desired way?" (the effectiveness problem)

SELECTION OF RESPONDENTS AND CASE MATERIALS

No serious problems in sampling were anticipated in this study as it was designed. The main objective was to get at the primary persons involved rather than to try to get only a "representative cross-section" of interview sources. In analysis of news items and coverage, both random and purposive selections were used so that both the most significant coverage problems and the representative ones could be stressed. During the most intensive period of study, in May and June, 1965, most of the news coverage analyzed was selected in advance—by studying decision days designated in advance rather than looking for selected examples "after the fact."

(Details on these and other methodological questions, plus examples of interview schedules, letters, and statements of objectives can be found, in part, in "Public Communication of U.S. Appellate Court Decisions," the author's unpublished doctoral dissertation at the University of Minnesota, which provided the starting point and much of the framework for this book.)

In total, roughly 75 persons were interviewed or contacted personally by mail during the main period of study in 1965/67. About two-thirds of these sources could be considered as semiformal or formal personal interviews—with members of the Supreme Court, Court staff, other judges, lawyers, law professors, government personnel, newsmen at the Court, and news executives away from the Court, all of whom were either directly or indirectly involved in this communications situation.

This list included contact with nearly all the principals. The most important refusal of an interview came from Chief Justice Earl Warren. This inability to communicate directly with the Chief Justice was a fairly serious drawback because of his obviously important role; but, fortunately, many of his attitudes on this subject could be pieced together from several published statements and from talking with others. (Details on the respondent problem can be found especially in "Interviewing at the Court," *Public Opinion Quarterly,* 31(Summer, 1967): 285–89.)

The only two other "serious non-respondents" were Paul Yost, Associated Press reporter at the Court during the most intensive period of field research, and former Press Officer Nelson (Ned) Potter. In total, the response rate was more than 90 per cent of those contacted for interviews by mail or in person.

INTERVIEWING PROCEDURES, OBSERVATION, AND CONTENT ANALYSES

The major sources relied on for methodological approaches are cited in the Selected Bibliography. Perhaps the main point worth stressing here is that the approach throughout the data-gathering was to seek broad patterns and analytical themes rather than minute quantifiable data. Even though basically qualitative, this study still sought to be as methodologically "sound" as possible—with efforts to control for interviewer bias, for example. The over-all objective in data collection was for as objective and systematic a critical analysis as seemed appropriate in a basically subjective area of study. While problems of validity and reliability, thus, could not be totally controlled, effort was made at least to be aware of these limitations.

Indeed, the exact limitation of the data gathered should be restated here. While this analysis has attempted to stress the communication patterns that are seemingly the most current and long-lasting, the study still is restricted because it was conducted primarily in 1965 and during only parts of 1966 and 1967. It must be acknowledged that changes may have taken place, or will take place, that might affect elements in this communication situation were it to be analyzed again tomorrow.

Appendix B

Case Analyses and Other News Stories

Page 1 News Story by Dana Bullen, the *Washington Star*, May 24, 1965:

HIGH COURT UPSETS LAW DELAYING RED MAIL

Unanimous Opinion Calls Act Infringement of First Amendment

A law authorizing the Post Office Department to hold up Communist mail was struck down today by the Supreme Court as an infringement of First Amendment rights.

Justice William O. Douglas, who delivered the court's 8–0 opinion, said the decision was based on the fact that an addressee was required to request that such detained mail be delivered.

"This requirement is almost certain to have a deterrent effect (on free expression)," Douglas said, "especially as respects those who have sensitive positions."

"Unconstitutional Abridgment"

"We rest on the narrow ground that the addressee in order to receive his mail must request in writing that it be delivered," Douglas

154

said. "This amounts . . . to an unconstitutional abridgment of the addressee's First Amendment rights."

Quoting from an earlier opinion by the late Justice Oliver Wendell Holmes, Douglas said ". . . the use of the mails is almost as much a part of free speech as the right to use our tongues. . . ."

The government contended the law served two basic purposes: It protected American citizens, especially those of recent foreign origin, from harassment; and it denied foreign powers the service of having the United States deliver their propaganda to people who did not want to receive it.

The law, attacked as contradictory to a free and open society and as an unwarranted invasion of privacy, provided that mailed matter, except in sealed letters, that originated in a foreign country and was determined by the Secretary of the Treasury to be Communist political propaganda was to be detained by the Postmaster General.

With certain exceptions this mail could be delivered only upon the addressee's request. If there was no request the mail was destroyed.

The Justices voted 8–0 in striking down the Post Office Department practice. Justice Byron R. White, former deputy attorney general, did not participate. Justices William J. Brennan, Arthur J. Goldberg and John M. Harlan filed a concurring opinion.

The court's action today affirmed a federal court ruling in a California case holding invalid sections of the law under which the Post Office Department was operating.

This case grew out of a suit filed by Leif Heilberg challenging constitutionality of the law after he was notified that the Post Office was holding up mail addressed to him entitled "A Proposal Concerning the International Communist Movement."

A Second Case

In a second case, the justices reversed a federal court ruling in New York dismissing a similar suit brought by Corliss Lamont, publisher of Basic Pamphlets, who had been sent a copy of the Peking Review.

In discussing the Post Office Department practice, Douglas said that any addressee "is likely to feel some inhibition in sending for literature which federal officials have condemned as 'Communist political propaganda.' "

"Public officials, like schoolteachers who have no tenure, might think they would invite disaster if they read what the federal government says contains the seeds of treason," Douglas said.

Douglas pointed out, however, that today's decision did not involve the extent to which Congress may classify mail or fix charges for carrying it.

The case also did not involve the right of customs officials to inspect for contraband or whether the Post Office Department's standard "could pass constitutional muster."

Astride Flow of Mail

The Court said that the 1962 act "sets administrative officials astride the flow of mail to inspect it, appraise it, write the addressee about it, and await a response before dispatching the mail."

In their concurring opinion, Brennan, Goldberg and Harlan emphasized that today's cases involved the rights of addressees rather than senders of mail.

"I think the right to receive publications is . . . a fundamental right," Brennan said. "It would be a barren marketplace of ideas that had only sellers and no buyers."

No Guaranteed Access

In the concurring opinion, Brennan said the First Amendment contains no specific guarantee of access to publications. However, he said, the protection of the Bill of Rights goes beyond specific guarantees to make such guarantees "fully meaningful."

Brennan rejected the argument that Post Office Department practice was justified "by the object of avoiding the subsidization of propaganda of foreign governments which bar American propaganda. . . ."

"If the government wishes to withdraw a subsidy or a privilege,"

Brennan said, "it must do so by means and on the terms which do not endanger First Amendment rights."

The court also had these other actions:

Sit-in Reversal

The high court summarily reversed, 6–3, a sit-in case in which a Georgia judge sentenced a young white coed to six months in jail and 12 months in a public works camp.

The maximum 18-month sentence was handed down by Fulton County Superior Court Judge Durwood T. Pye in February, 1964, for Miss Mardon R. Walker, 18, of East Greenwich, R.I.

A brief unsigned order cited the Supreme Court's earlier decision that the 1964 Civil Rights Act wiped out sit-in prosecutions still pending before trial or appellate courts.

Miss Walker, the daughter of a Navy captain at the Pentagon, was an exchange student from Connecticut College for Women at predominantly Negro Spelman College in Atlanta at the time of the incident.

Labor Law Review

The court agreed to review a ruling that a federal court could not hear a libel suit growing out of a union organizing campaign because of the preempting jurisdiction of the National Labor Relations Board over labor matters.

The case involves a suit by a Pinkerton detective agency official against a union that sought to organize Pinkerton employes in 1962. The U.S. 6th Circuit Court of Appeals held that a lower federal court lacked jurisdiction to hear the libel case.

Television Disclosure

The court unanimously upheld the Federal Communications Commission's authority to require public disclosure of information about the television industry in investigative proceedings except where parties seeking non-public sessions show that the public interest, proper dispatch of business or the ends of justice warrant such private sessions.

The justices acted on an appeal by the FCC from a ruling of the U.S. 9th Circuit Court of Appeals in San Francisco that information given the FCC should be held confidential unless the commission showed a court in an adversary proceeding good cause to divulge it.

HOME REPAIRS

The tribunal refused to review a $100,000 criminal contempt fine imposed by the U.S. 7th Circuit Court of Appeals on the Holland Furnace Co., Holland, Mich., for failing to halt court-banned furnace repair practices.

The firm, now under new management, was ordered by the court in 1959 to stop representing its employes as inspectors, dismantling furnaces without permission and misrepresenting the condition of dismantled furnaces.

The company's appeal said the $100,000 fine appeared to be the largest penalty ever imposed for violation of an order by the Federal Trade Commission. The Circuit Court order had been to enforce the FTC ruling.

The appeal said the prohibited activities were halted in 1962 when new management took over the firm. It said the fine would hurt innocent creditors. The fine covered activities before the 1962 change in management.

ASSOCIATED PRESS NEWS WIRE COPY, MAY 24, 1965 (Separate Communist Mail Case Story)

(The wire services' stories reproduced here were originally transmitted in the standard teletype format of all-capital letters. They have been edited without changing their content for better readability. The all-capital-letters style, mechanical transmission errors, and special editors' notations for each segment of copy sent during the day have been deleted.)

WASHINGTON, May 24 (AP)—The Supreme Court struck down today a 1962 law authorizing the Post Office Department to hold up Communist mail from abroad.

Justice William O. Douglas delivered the 8–0 decision. Justice Byron R. White took no part.

The government contended the law served two basic purposes: it protected American citizens, especially those of recent foreign origin, from harassment; it denied foreign powers the service of having the United States deliver their propaganda to people who did not want to receive it.

The law was attacked as contradictory to a free and open society and as an unwarranted invasion of privacy.

The law provided that mailed matter, except sealed letters, that originated in a foreign country and was determined by the Secretary of the Treasury to be Communist political propaganda was to be detained by the Postmaster General.

With certain exceptions this mail could be delivered only upon the addressee's request. If there was no request the mail was destroyed.

Douglas said the Court had to conclude that the act as construed and applied is unconstitutional "because it requires an official act (viz. returning a reply card) as a limitation on the unfettered exercise of the addressee's First Amendment right."

Douglas said the Court had rested its decision "on the narrow ground that the addressee in order to receive his mail must request in writing that it be delivered."

"This amounts in our judgment to an unconstitutional abridgement of the addressee's First Amendment rights," he said. "The addressee carries an affirmative obligation which we do not think the government may impose on him. This requirement is almost certain to have a deterrent effect, especially as respects those who have sensitive positions. Their livelihood may be dependent on a security clearance."

The Court ruled in two separate but parallel cases.

In one, Corliss Lamont, who publishes and distributes pamphlets and other literature, appealed to the Supreme Court from a decision by a special three-judge federal court in New York City.

Lamont had been notified in July, 1963, that a copy of a Peking review was being held as "Communist political propaganda." Without responding to the notice, he started his suit.

The Post Office Department then informed Lamont that start of the suit showed he wanted to receive the mail. The federal court agreed in the sense that it held the case to be moot.

The mail case also was brought to the Supreme Court by the Justice Department, which appealed a decision by a three-judge federal court in San Francisco that the law is unconstitutional.

In this case, Leif Heilberg, a citizen of Denmark who said he was considering applying for U.S. citizenship, objected to delay of mail from Communist countries that he received as a member of the Universal Esperanto Association.

Like Lamont, he refused to request delivery after the Post Office notified him a piece of mail was being held back. And, as in Lamont's case, the Post Office informed him that filing of a suit expressed a desire to receive his mail. But unlike the federal court in New York, the California court decided the case was not moot and declared the law unconstitutional as an infringement of the First Amendment's guarantee of free speech.

UNITED PRESS INTERNATIONAL NEWS WIRE COPY,
    MAY 24, 1965
(Separate Communist Mail Case Story)

WASHINGTON, May 24 (UPI)—The Supreme Court today knocked down as unconstitutional a 1962 law restricting U.S. mail deliveries of Communist political propaganda from abroad.

The law provides among other things that such mail cannot be delivered unless the addressee requests it in writing. The Court found this an abridgement of First Amendment rights.

"The addressee carries an affirmative obligation which we do not think the government may impose on him," said Justice William O. Douglas, who spoke for the Court.

Justice Byron R. White did not participate in the case. Justices William J. Brennan, Jr., Arthur J. Goldberg and John M. Harlan concurred with Douglas in a separate opinion.

Douglas said persons in "sensitive positions" would naturally be reluctant to sign for literature deemed communistic.

"Public officials, like school teachers who have no tenure, might think they would invite disaster if they read what the federal government says contains the seeds of treason," he said.

The Court acted in cases from New York and San Francisco.

The first was appealed by Corliss Lamont, who does business in New York under the name Basic Pamphlets. A special three-judge federal panel dismissed his challenge of the law on May 19, 1964.

The other case was brought to the high court by the Justice Department after a three-judge court found the statute unconstitutional in a test brought by Leif Heilberg of San Francisco.

The statute was designed to curb an influx of foreign propaganda. It provides that the Bureau of Customs shall determine what countries come within the specifications laid down in the law.

Foreign mail determined to be Communist propaganda is not delivered, except to libraries and the like, unless the addressee signs a card from the Post Office.

Lamont sued after he was asked whether he wanted to receive "Peking Review No. 12, 1963." He said he did not want his mail detained nor did he wish his name on a list of persons desiring to receive Communist propaganda.

At this point, the Post Office decided to forward all his mail without any signed cards.

The Justice Department told the Supreme Court the Post Office has decided not to keep any lists in connection with the law.

ASSOCIATED PRESS WIRE COPY, JUNE 1, 1965,
FOR JUNE 2, 1965
(Lead only of roundup story)

WASHINGTON, June 1 (AP)—The Supreme Court ruled today on legislative reapportionment disputes in New York, Illinois, California and Idaho involving widely different aspects of its "one-man, one-vote" decree.

The Court, preparing to start its summer recess after next Monday's decision day, cleared up without hearing arguments all of its pending reapportionment cases by:

—Refusing 8 to 1 to hold up a special election in New York State next November 2. A Federal District Court ordered the election over objections by the State Supreme Court that 15 more legislators would be elected than the 150 the State Constitution prescribes.

The dissenter, Justice John M. Harlan, wanted to grant a quick high court hearing on the issue, declaring, "I am wholly at a loss to understand the Court's casual way of disposing of this matter and I can find no considerations of any kind which justifies it.

"The Court should be willing to face up articulately to these difficult problems which have followed as a not unnatural aftermath of its reapportionment decisions of last term."

—Ruling 8 to 0 that the federal court in Illinois step aside for a reasonable time but keep watch to give the state agencies a chance to redistrict the Illinois State Senate on a population basis. The high court said states should be encouraged to act on their own in such matters.

—Upholding unanimously—but three justices "reluctantly"—a federal court order that California must reapportion its Senate by July 1 on a population basis even though the state's voters three times have rejected reports to change the present alignment.

—Unanimously refusing to intervene in a suit by two Idaho citizens challenging the fairness of the state's new legislative reapportionment law passed on March 25.

In the civil rights field, the Court acted on major appeals by:

—Agreeing to review at its next term the dismissal of federal conspiracy indictments against six Georgia men accused in the shotgun slaying near Athens, Georgia, last July 11 of Lemuel A. Penn, District of Columbia Negro educator. This appeal challenges a ruling by U.S. District Judge W. M. Bootle of Macon, Georgia, that the Justice Department had failed to show violation of federal law.

—Rejecting an appeal from U.S. District Judge W. Harold Cox of

Jackson, Mississippi, that it uphold his contempt citation of U.S. District Attorney Robert E. Hauberg for his refusal to sign an indictment of two Negroes in a 1964 voter registration suit. The high court merely refused to review a circuit court decision overturning Cox's contempt citation.

—Refusing 7 to 2 to review the disorderly conduct convictions of three white persons and a Negro arrested at a civil rights demonstration in an amusement park near Baltimore in 1959.

Gwynn Oak Park has since dropped its policy of racial segregation. The four demonstrators were arrested after refusing the request of a law officer to leave the park.

The Supreme Court dismissed the appeal in a brief order saying it did so for "want of jurisdiction."

But the dissenters, Chief Justice Earl Warren and William O. Douglas, agreed with lawyers for the four demonstrators that the 1964 Civil Rights Act wiped out the convictions. Warren said:

"Clearly, nothing petitioners did prior to being placed under arrest could be called disorderly conduct: their only 'sins' to that point were being Negro or being in the company of Negroes, and politely refusing to leave the park. . . .

"In two recent decisions we have, rightly in my opinion, recognized that people denied service because of their race are likely to react with less than wholehearted cooperation. Today, I fear, the Court forgets that elemental principle of human conduct and demands, on paying of criminal penalties, the patience of Job. . . ."

UNITED PRESS INTERNATIONAL WIRE COPY,
  JUNE 1, 1965, FOR JUNE 2, 1965
(Lead only of roundup story)

WASHINGTON, June 1 (UPI)—The Supreme Court today strongly encouraged state courts to take greater responsibility in settling their own legislative reapportionment disputes.

The urging came in an Illinois case where both the State Supreme Court and a three-judge federal panel had asserted jurisdiction in reapportioning the State Senate.

Ruling in favor of the state court in the conflict, the Supreme Court declared:

"The power of the judiciary of a state to require valid reapportionment or to formulate a valid redistricting plan has not only been recognized by this court but appropriate action by the states in such cases has been specifically encouraged."

The brief, unsigned opinion was one of four reapportionment actions taken by the Court. The other cases involved California, New York and Idaho.

Here is what the Court did on those:

California—reaffirmed a decision by a special three-judge federal court that the California Senate, now apportioned along geographic and county lines, must be based solely on population in keeping with the "one-man, one-vote" decision of last year. Justices John M. Harlan, Tom C. Clark and Potter Stewart dissented, noting that proposals to change the present system had been turned down by California voters in 1948, 1960, and 1962.

New York—refused to interfere with a lower court order requiring a special election of the New York Legislature on November 2. The state's highest court had ruled that the plan under which the election would be conducted would violate the State Constitution. Nonetheless the Supreme Court refused without comment to grant a stay at this point. Harlan filed an emphatic dissent.

Idaho—referred back to a federal court in Boise a controversy over reapportionment in that state. The Supreme Court said that voter complaints and state officials should seek action at the lower level in light of the fact that the State Legislature passed a reapportionment bill before adjourning in March.

The background of the Illinois case:

On January 22, the three-judge federal panel barred redistricting by any branch of the state government except by the Legislature.

On February 4, the State Supreme Court claimed jurisdiction and said it had the responsibility of acting if the Legislature did not.

State Attorney General William G. Clark asked the Supreme Court to uphold the federal jurisdiction.

But today the Court vacated the federal court order and assigned priority to the State Supreme Court justices.

It directed the lower Federal Court to allow reasonable time in which "appropriate agencies of the State of Illinois, including its Supreme Court, may validly redistrict the Illinois State Senate."

If no action was taken, today's opinion said, the federal judges then could go ahead with an apportionment plan of their own or order an at-large election in 1966—but only if the state could not settle its own problem. . . .

Associated Press Wire Copy, June 7, 1965, for June 8, 1965
(Separate story on Estes TV Case)

WASHINGTON, June 7 (AP)—The Supreme Court today threw out Billie Sol Estes' conviction on a Texas swindling charge because his trial was televised.

The historical decision split the Court as it wrestled for the first time with the question whether a defendant can get a fair trial under the eye of television cameras.

By the narrowest margin, 5 to 4, it ruled that in Estes' case he couldn't. But two justices explicitly said no sweeping meaning should be read into today's opinion.

The television networks withheld comment on the Court's ruling pending full reading of the several opinions.

But the General Counsel of the National Association of Broadcasters, Douglas A. Anello, expressed "extreme disappointment" over the ruling. However, he added, "We are encouraged by the words of Mr. Justice Brennan that 'today's decision is not a blanket constitutional prohibition against the televising of state criminal trials.'"

The Texas judge who permitted the televising insisted today that he feels such coverage does not prejudice a defendant's rights if it is carefully supervised.

The reversal affected only a state conviction of Estes, a one-time millionaire West Texas promoter. It did not touch a federal mail-fraud conviction under which he is now serving a 15-year sentence in the penitentiary at Leavenworth, Kansas.

Among the questions left unanswered by the Court's decision is whether the case will have any effect on televising of Congressional hearings in which witnesses might be subject to later criminal trials.

This was the high tribunal's last sitting before summer recess, which ends next October 4. . . .

United Press International Wire Copy, June 7, 1965, for June 8, 1965
(Separate story on Estes TV Case)

WASHINGTON, June 7 (UPI)—The Supreme Court, breaking new judicial ground, today barred television and radio coverage of heavily publicized and highly sensational trials as a violation of a defendant's constitutional rights to a fair trial.

In a 5–4 decision, the Court reversed the October, 1962, conviction of Texas financier Billie Sol Estes on a charge of swindling. Portions of the county district court trial at Tyler, Texas, were televised and broadcast on radio.

Estes had appealed the conviction, which led to an eight-year jail sentence, for this reason.

Today's high court decision will not affect the 15-year sentence Estes now is serving at Ft. Leavenworth, Kansas, on a Federal conviction for mail fraud and conspiracy in March, 1963.

The majority opinion, written by Justice Tom C. Clark of Texas, said television cameras in the courtroom could be unfair to a defendant and exceed the limits of freedom of the press guaranteed in the First Amendment.

"The heightened public clamor resulting from radio and television coverage will inevitably result in prejudice," he said. "Trial by television is, therefore, foreign to our system."

The Court ruled on the ground that Estes had been denied due process of law as provided in the 14th Amendment.

Never before had the Supreme Court considered the issue of television in the courtroom. Federal rules of cardinal procedure already prohibit televising of court trials.

Television coverage is permitted in the courts of only two states—Texas and Colorado—and then at the judge's discretion. The other states follow Canon 35 of the American Bar Association (ABA), which opposes photographing, televising or broadcasting of court proceedings.

Appendix C

Example of Case Memorandum
Prepared by Law Professors

ASSOCIATION OF AMERICAN LAW SCHOOLS
Committee on Supreme Court Decisions

Analysis prepared by Paul W. Bruton
March 26, 1965

BILLIE SOL ESTES v. THE STATE OF TEXAS
Docket No. 256
(On certiorari to The Court of Criminal Appeals of Texas)

This case raises for the first time in the Supreme Court of the United States the following question: May a criminal defendant be

---

This is one of a series of memoranda being prepared [in advance of the Supreme Court's final written decision] under the auspices of the Association of American Law Schools with the aim of contributing to a better public understanding of the work of the United States Supreme Court. The memoranda are for the exclusive use of representatives of the press, radio, and television, who will receive copies by mail upon written request to the Association of American Law Schools, 1521 New Hampshire Avenue, N.W., Washington, D.C. 20036. No part of this memoranda has any approval by the Supreme Court or any other branch or office of the government. Not for any attribution to the Association of American Law Schools or the author without specific authorization. Reprinted with permission of the author, Paul W. Bruton, and the AALS.

compelled against his will to submit to the broadcasting of his trial by television to the public?

A. *Significance of the case.*

Thus is brought to the Supreme Court an important contemporary aspect of the much debated question of fair trial versus free expression. Two approaches to the question are highlighted by the difference between the canons of judicial ethics adopted by the American Bar Association on one hand, and those adopted by The Integrated Bar of Texas, on the other. Judicial Canon 35 of the American Bar Association states that the taking of photographs, broadcasting or televising of court proceedings "detract from the essential dignity of the proceedings, distract participants and witnesses in giving testimony and create misconceptions with respect thereto in the mind of the public and should not be permitted."

Judicial Canon 28 of the Texas Bar takes the position that photography, broadcasting and televising of court proceedings are not detrimental or distracting if properly supervised and controlled. Such supervision and control is left to the trial judge but it is stated that (1) there should be no use of flash bulbs or other artificial lighting and (2) no witness, over his objection, should be photographed or televised, nor should his voice be broadcast without his permission.

The petitioner (defendant below) contends that the Constitution of the United States (specifically the due process and equal protection clauses of the Fourteenth Amendment) requires that a trial judge follow the practice recommended by the American Bar Association at least when the defendant requests.

B. *The Facts of the Case.*

The criminal prosecution of Billie Sol Estes for certain alleged frauds attracted a great deal of public attention. The prosecution was initiated by indictment filed July 20, 1962, in Reeves County, Texas, and was transferred to the City of Tyler in Smith County where it was set for trial on September 24, 1962. Having learned that the court intended to permit live telecasting of the trial, defendant's counsel on September 24 objected to such procedure and moved for a continuance. After proceedings which extended into the 25th, the case was continued, but the motion against photographs, television and broadcasting was denied.

The proceedings of September 24 and 25 were covered by live television as well as other media. The scene of the courthouse at that time was reported in the *New York Times* for September 25, 1962, as follows:

"A television motor van, big as an intercontinental bus, was parked outside the courthouse and second floor courtroom was a forest of equipment. Two television cameras had been set up, inside the bar and four marked cameras were aligned outside the gates. A microphone stuck its 12-inch snout inside the jury box, now occupied by an overflow of reporters from the press table and three microphones confronted Judge Dunagan on his bench. Cables and wires snaked over the floor."

Continuance was granted until October 22 and by that time the situation had been changed. A booth had been constructed in the rear of the courtroom; presumably to make the booth inconspicuous, it was painted the same color as the courtroom. A small opening at the top was used to give the cameras a view of the proceedings. During the trial the court permitted telecasting by ABC, NBC, CBS, and a local station, KRLD. The telecasting, which produced no sound in the courtroom, was done on film at intervals, but the live telecasting was limited to the argument of the prosecution, and the return of the jury's verdict and its acceptance by the court. Defense counsel's request that his argument not be telecast was observed. Defendant did not testify nor did he call any witnesses; no juror or witness requested that he not be televised.

Defendant was convicted and his conviction affirmed by the Court of Criminal Appeals.

C. The opposing arguments.

1. Petitioner contends that he was denied due process of law and the equal protection of the laws because the trial court over his objection required him to submit to live television coverage of his trial; he states that he was "needlessly humiliated and commercially exhibited;" he asserts that the total potential audience was 760,000 and approximately 100,000 persons viewed the broadcast; he further

asserts that the television interfered with his adequate representation by counsel; he contends that only two states (Texas and Colorado) do not follow ABA Canon 35.

2. The state denies that due process or equal protection of the laws has been violated and emphasizes the following circumstances: because of the manner in which the cameras were concealed and the lack of noise from their operation, the decorum of the courtroom was not disturbed; since the petitioner did not testify or call any witnesses, neither he nor his witnesses were burdened by the presence of the cameras; since defense counsel's argument at the trial was not televised, there is no basis for finding that representation by counsel was interfered with in any way; there is no evidence on any possible effect on the jury.

D. *Relation of the case to prior decisions.*

All of the previous decisions of the Supreme Court involving the reporting of criminal proceedings have concerned pre-trial publicity which it was claimed affected or could have affected the conduct of the trial adversely to the defendant. In *Stroble v. California* 343 U.S. 181 (1952) and *Irvin v. Dowd*, 366 U.S. 717 (1961) there was newspaper publicity before trial of a character likely to prejudice the community against the defendant. The conviction was allowed to stand in *Stroble* because there was no showing that the jury had been prejudiced, while in *Irvin* the conviction was reversed on the ground that the community had been so inflamed against the defendant that he had been denied his constitutional right to a trial by a fair and impartial jury. In the more recent case of *Ridean v. Louisiana,* 373 U.S. 723 (1963), the conviction was also reversed because of a pretrial broadcast of a filmed "interview" between the defendant and the sheriff in which the defendant admitted he had committed the alleged crimes. A majority of the Court thought that defendant had been denied due process of law because he was tried by a jury drawn from the community which had seen the broadcast, although only three of the jurors had seen it and they asserted they could give their verdict solely on the basis of evidence presented at the trial.

The *Ridean* case may evidence a trend in the Court's opinions in the direction of greater control of pre-trial publicity because of its potentially prejudicial character, but it gives little clue as to what the decision will be in the Estes case where the potential effect on the jury is either non-existent or minimal.

E. *The issues in the case and their possible disposition.*

1. One basic question is: Did the television coverage, as controlled in this case, threaten in any way the defendant's right to a fair and impartial trial? If so, the above cases could support a decision that defendant was denied due process of law. But the state strenuously contends that as the television was operated (outlined in paragraph C 2 above), it could have had no possible adverse effect on the fairness of the trial. If the court agrees with this contention, the above cases (paragraph D) can readily be distinguished and the conclusion reached that the defendant's due process rights to a fair trial were in no way infringed.

2. A further contention, which the court may consider, is that the televising or broadcasting of trials would generally have an adverse effect on the administration of justice. Aside from interfering with the decorum of the courtroom, if not carefully controlled, such media of communication may have a tendency to make a public spectacle of judicial proceedings and by highlighting sensational episodes convey misleading conceptions of the work of the courts; broadcasting or televising may also induce judges, lawyers, witnesses and jurors to "play to the public." Consideration of this kind lay back of the ABA Canon 35 and Rule 53 of the Federal Rules of Criminal Procedure which bars the taking of photographs or the radio broadcasting of trials in the federal courts. On behalf of Estes it is argued that such considerations support a rule of due process which would uniformly ban the televising of trials regardless of the effect in any particular case. However, the Supreme Court may view this as a matter of judicial administration within control of the courts involved and not a constitutional rule which a criminal defendant may invoke.

3. A third question is whether a criminal defendant has some kind of limited "right to privacy" to the effect that his misfortune shall not be made a public spectacle or "commercialized" over the air. Consideration of this point must take cognizance of the fact that crimi-

nal trials are traditionally public as recognized by the Sixth Amendment of the United States Constitution.

4. A final issue is whether a federally imposed prohibition on the televising of criminal trials would infringe the constitutionally protected freedom of communication by the news media. However, the acceptance of this argument would place in jeopardy the constitutional validity of ABA Canon 35 (voluntarily adopted by the courts of most of the states) and Rule 53 of the Federal Rules of Criminal Procedure. It has long been assumed that whatever the rights of the news media with reference to the reporting of trials, those rights do not include the privilege to photograph, broadcast or televise judicial proceedings.

Appendix D

Example of Clarifying Opinion
by a Supreme Court Justice

381 U.S. 532, 617

No. 256.—October Term, 1964

Billie Sol Estes, Petitioner,	On Writ of Certiorari to the
v.	Court of Criminal Appeals
State of Texas	of Texas

(June 7, 1965)

MR. JUSTICE BRENNAN.

I write merely to emphasize that only four of the five Justices voting to reverse rest on the proposition that televised criminal trials are constitutionally infirm, whatever the circumstances. Although the opinion announced by my Brother Clark purports to be "an opinion of the Court," my Brother Harlan subscribes to a significantly less sweeping proposition. He states:

"The *Estes* trial was a heavily publicized and highly sensational affair. I therefore put aside all other types of cases. . . . The resolution of those further questions should await an appropriate case; the Court should proceed only step by step in this unplowed field. *The opinion of the Court necessarily goes no further, for only the four members of the majority who unreservedly join the Court's opinion would resolve those questions now.*" Ante, p————. (Emphasis supplied.)

174

Thus today's decision is *not* a blanket constitutional prohibition against the televising of state criminal trials.

While I join the dissents of my Brothers Stewart and White, I do so on the understanding that their use of the expressions "the Court's opinion" or "the opinion of the Court" refers only to those views of our four Brethren which my Brother Harlan explicitly states he shares.

Selected Bibliography

A. A Bibliographic Note

ANY SELECTED LIST of references needs a brief explanation as to the rationale behind their selection. In addition, a summary statement of the main types of sources used would be appropriate.

The main published writings relating to Court news coverage problems are, clearly, the articles by Hachten, Newland, Cranberg, and Carroll and the chapter by Clayton from Hiebert's *The Press in Washington*. (Specific citations for all of these and other bibliographic notations can be found on pp. 177–89.)

In the total context of Washington news coverage, the most relevant sources would be, besides Hiebert: Rivers' *The Opinionmakers;* Cater's *The Fourth Branch of Government*, and especially Cohen's *The Press and Foreign Policy*. The Cohen book, in fact, is probably the single most significant analytical source used. This study of Court communication problems attempts, where possible, to show comparability of findings or extensions of the data between the two news fields of law and foreign relations.

Most sources relied on can be found through footnotes and specific references throughout the book. In general, then, the selected bibliography should be considered as the basic list of works most useful or stimulating for research methodology, background information, and study of the overriding communications theme. The references in

176

law and the legal process, in particular, are listed with this idea of general indebtedness—not inclusiveness.

Although this book does not aim in itself to enlighten lay readers about what the Supreme Court is or how it works, a brief comment about this type of writing would seem appropriate. Interestingly, two of the most insightful books in this category are by former Court newsmen—*The Making of Justice* by Clayton and *Gideon's Trumpet* by Lewis (also partly rewritten as *The Supreme Court and How It Works*, one of a series on American government for younger people). Lewis' many articles explaining the Court (especially in the *New York Times Magazine*) also are noteworthy. There are many other such sources that might be cited here, but perhaps potentially the most helpful is *Equal Justice Under Law*, put out by the Foundation of the Federal Bar Association and printed in cooperation with the National Geographic Society.

It is also important here to stress what the Selected Bibliography does *not* include. In particular, there is no single list of all persons interviewed or contacted by mail. One main reason is to protect those who requested that some or all of their comments not be attributed to them. Most of the persons interviewed or corresponded with are included in footnotes; these types of sources are also discussed briefly and generally in Appendix A.

Also omitted are full lists of case materials and news stories studied. Besides the difficulties presented by sheer numbers, mere lists of publications and Court cases analyzed here would be relatively meaningless without extensive annotation as to what each item involved or was used for. Thus, again, heavy reliance for specific sources is placed on footnoting and the Index.

In sum, then, the selected bibliography does not attempt to be all-encompassing but simply attempts to stress the major secondary sources in the literature which had the most influence on this communications analysis.

B. Books and Collections of Readings

Abraham, Henry J. *The Judiciary*. Boston: Allyn and Bacon, 1965.
Adams, Henry. *The Education of Henry Adams*. Boston: Houghton Mifflin Co., 1918.

Angell, Robert C. *Free Society & Moral Crisis.* Ann Arbor: University of Michigan Press, 1958.

Auerbach, Carl, *et al. The Legal Process.* San Francisco: Chandler Pub. Co., 1961.

Bauer, Raymond A.; Pool, Ithiel de Sola; and Dexter, Lewis A. *American Business and Public Policy.* New York: Atherton Press, 1963.

Berelson, Bernard, and Janowitz, Morris (eds.). *Reader in Public Opinion and Communication.* New York: Free Press, 1953 and 1966.

————, and Steiner, Gary A. *Human Behavior.* New York: Harcourt, Brace & World, 1964.

Blanshard, Paul. *Religion and the Schools.* Boston: Beacon Press, 1963.

Boorstin, Daniel J. *The Image.* New York: Harper and Row, 1961.

Bryson, Lyman (ed.). *The Communication of Ideas.* New York: Harper & Brothers, 1948.

Cardozo, Benjamin N. *The Nature of the Judicial Process.* New Haven: Yale University Press, 1921.

Cater, Douglass. *The Fourth Branch of Government.* Boston: Houghton Mifflin Co., 1959.

Chase, Stuart. *Power of Words.* New York: Harcourt, Brace and Co., 1954.

Clayton, James E. *The Making of Justice.* New York: E. P. Dutton & Co., 1964.

Cohen, Bernard C. *The Press and Foreign Policy.* Princeton, N. J.: Princeton University Press, 1963.

Commission on Freedom of the Press. *A Free and Responsible Press.* Chicago: University of Chicago Press, 1947.

Corwin, Edward S. *The Constitution and What It Means Today.* New York: Atheneum, 1963.

Dahl, Robert A. *A Preface to Democratic Theory.* Chicago: University of Chicago Press, 1956.

Deutsch, Karl W. *The Nerves of Government.* New York: Free Press, 1963.

Dexter, Lewis A., and White, David M. (eds.). *People, Society, and Mass Communications.* New York: Free Press of Glencoe, 1964.

Dicey, A. V. *Lectures on the Relation Between Law and Public Opinion in England.* London: Macmillan & Co., 1924.

Fagen, Richard R. *Politics and Communication.* Boston: Little, Brown and Co., 1966.

Faris, Robert E. L. (ed.). *Handbook of Modern Sociology.* Chicago: Rand McNally Co., 1964.

Ferry, W. H., and Ashmore, Harry S. *Mass Communications.* Santa Barbara, Calif.: Center for the Study of Democratic Institutions, 1966.

Foundation of the Federal Bar Association. *Equal Justice Under Law.* Washington, D.C.: Foundation of the Federal Bar Association, 1965.

Frank, Jerome. *Courts on Trial.* Princeton, N. J.: Princeton University Press, 1949.

————. *Law and the Modern Mind.* New York: Brentano's, 1930.

Frank, John P. *Marble Palace*. New York: Alfred A. Knopf, 1958.

————. *The Warren Court*. New York: Macmillan Co., 1964.

Frankfurter, Felix. *Mr. Justice Holmes and the Supreme Court*. Cambridge, Mass.: Harvard University Press, 1938.

————, and Landis, James M. *The Business of the Supreme Court*. New York: Macmillan Co., 1927.

Freund, Paul A. *On Understanding the Supreme Court*. Boston: Little, Brown and Co., 1949.

Gerald, J. Edward. *The Social Responsibility of the Press*. Minneapolis: University of Minnesota Press, 1963.

Gross, Gerald (ed.). *The Responsibility of the Press*. New York: Fleet Publishing Corp., 1966.

Hall, Edward T. *The Silent Language*. New York: Premier Book, 1959.

Hiebert, Ray Eldon (ed.). *The Press in Washington*. New York: Dodd, Mead & Co., 1966.

Hocking, William E. *Freedom of the Press*. Chicago: University of Chicago Press, 1947.

Hughes, Charles Evans. *The Supreme Court of the United States*. New York: Columbia University Press, 1928.

Hyneman, Charles S. *The Supreme Court on Trial*. New York: Atherton Press, 1963.

Innis, Harold. *The Bias of Communication*. Toronto: University of Toronto Press, 1951.

Jackson, Robert H. *The Struggle for Judicial Supremacy*. New York: Alfred A. Knopf, 1941.

————. *The Supreme Court in the American System of Government*. New York: Harper Torchbooks, 1963.

Jacob, Herbert. *Justice in America*. Boston: Little, Brown and Co., 1965.

Kahn, Robert L., and Cannell, Charles F. *The Dynamics of Interviewing*. New York: John Wiley & Sons, 1957.

Kaplan, Abraham. *The Conduct of Inquiry*. San Francisco: Chandler Pub. Co., 1964.

Key, V. O., Jr. *Public Opinion and American Democracy*. New York: Alfred A. Knopf, 1961.

Klapper, Joseph T. *The Effects of Mass Communication*. Glencoe, Ill.: Free Press of Glencoe, 1960.

Krislov, Samuel. *The Supreme Court in the Political Process*. New York: Macmillan Co., 1965.

Lane, Robert E., and David O. Sears. *Public Opinion*. Englewood Cliffs, N.J.: Prentice-Hall, 1964.

Lasswell, Harold D. *The Future of Political Science*. New York: Atherton Press, 1963.

Lazarsfeld, Paul F., and Stanton, Frank M. (eds.). *Communications Research*. New York: Harper & Brothers, 1949.

Levi, Edward H. *An Introduction to Legal Reasoning.* Chicago: University of Chicago Press, 1948.

Lewis, Anthony. *Gideon's Trumpet.* New York: Random House, 1964.

————. *The Supreme Court and How It Works.* New York: Random House, 1966.

Liebling, A. J. *The Press.* New York: Ballantine Books, 1961.

Lindstrom, Carl E. *The Fading American Newspaper.* Garden City, N.Y.: Doubleday & Co., 1960.

Lindzey, Gardner (ed.). *Handbook of Social Psychology.* Vols. I and II. Cambridge, Mass.: Addison-Wesley Pub. Co., 1954.

Lippmann, Walter. *Essays in the Public Philosophy.* Boston: Little, Brown and Co., 1955.

————. *Public Opinion.* New York: Macmillan Co., 1922 (1960 edition).

Lipset, Seymour M.; Trow, Martin A.; and Coleman, James S. *Union Democracy.* Garden City, N.Y.: Anchor Books, 1962.

Llewellyn, Karl N. *The Bramble Bush.* New York: Oceana Publications, 1960.

Martindale, Don. *The Nature and Types of Sociological Theory.* Boston: Houghton Mifflin Co., 1960.

Mason, Alpheus T. *Harlan Fiske Stone, Pillar of the Law.* New York: Viking Press, 1956.

————. *William Howard Taft: Chief Justice.* New York: Simon and Schuster, 1965.

————, and Beaney, William M. *American Constitutional Law.* Englewood Cliffs, N. J.: Prentice-Hall, 1964.

Matthews, Donald R. *U.S. Senators and Their World.* Chapel Hill, N.C.: University of North Carolina Press, 1960.

Mayers, Lewis. *The American Legal System.* New York: Harper & Row, 1964.

McCloskey, Robert G. *The American Supreme Court.* Chicago: University of Chicago Press, 1960.

Mead, George H. *Mind, Self and Society.* Chicago: University of Chicago Press, 1934.

Merton, Robert K. *Social Theory and Social Structure.* Glencoe, Ill.: Free Press of Glencoe, 1957.

Milbrath, Lester. *The Washington Lobbyists.* Chicago: Rand McNally, 1963.

Morris, Clarence. *How Lawyers Think.* Cambridge, Mass.: Harvard University Press, 1937.

Murphy, Walter F. *Elements of Judicial Strategy.* Chicago: University of Chicago Press, 1964.

————, and Pritchett, C. Herman. *Courts, Judges, and Politics.* New York: Random House, 1961.

Nafziger, Ralph O., and White, David M. (eds.). *Introduction to Mass*

Communications Research. Baton Rouge: Louisiana State University Press, 1963.

Nimmo, Dan D. *Newsgathering in Washington*. New York: Atherton Press, 1964.

Peltason, J. W. *Federal Courts in the Political Process*. Garden City, N.Y.: Doubleday & Co., 1955.

————. *Fifty-Eight Lonely Men*. New York: Harcourt, Brace & World, 1961.

Peterson, Theodore; Jensen, Jay W.; and Rivers, William L. *The Mass Media and Modern Society*. New York: Holt, Rinehart & Winston, 1965.

Pritchett, C. Herman. *The American Constitution*. New York: McGraw-Hill, 1959.

————. *Congress Versus the Supreme Court*. Minneapolis: University of Minnesota Press, 1961.

Reston, James. *The Artillery of the Press*. New York: Harper & Row, 1966.

Rivers, William L. *The Opinionmakers*. Boston: Beacon Press, 1965.

Roche, John P., and Levy, Leonard W. *The Judiciary*. New York: Harcourt, Brace & World, 1964.

Rosenblum, Victor G. *Law as a Political Instrument*. New York: Random House, 1955.

Rosten, Leo C. *The Washington Correspondents*. New York: Harcourt, Brace and Co., 1937.

Rourke, Francis E. *Secrecy and Publicity*. Baltimore: Johns Hopkins Press, 1961.

Schmidhauser, John R. (ed.). *Constitutional Law in the Political Process*. Chicago: Rand McNally, 1963.

————. *The Supreme Court*. New York: Holt, Rinehart and Winston, 1960.

Schramm, Wilbur (ed.). *Mass Communications*. Urbana: University of Illinois Press, 1960.

————. *Responsibility in Mass Communication*. New York: Harper & Brothers, 1957.

———— (ed.). *The Process and Effects of Mass Communication*. Urbana: University of Illinois Press, 1954.

———— (ed.). *The Science of Human Communication*. New York: Basic Books, 1963.

Schubert, Glendon A. (ed.). *Judicial Behavior*. Chicago: Rand McNally, 1964.

———— (ed.). *Judicial Decision-Making*. New York: Free Press of Glencoe, 1963.

Selltiz, Claire, *et al. Research Methods in Social Relations*. New York: Holt, Rinehart & Winston, 1961.

Shannon, Claude E., and Weaver, Warren. *The Mathematical Theory of Communication*. Urbana: University of Illinois Press, 1949.
Siebert, Fred S.; Peterson, Theodore; and Schramm, Wilbur. *Four Theories of the Press*. Urbana: University of Illinois Press, 1956.
Swisher, Carl B. *The Growth of Constitutional Power in the United States*. Chicago: Phoenix Books, 1963.
————. *The Supreme Court in Modern Role*. New York: New York University Press, 1958 and 1965.
Truman, David. *The Governmental Process*. New York: Alfred A. Knopf, 1951.
Warren, Charles. *The Supreme Court in U.S. History*. Vols. I and II. Boston: Little, Brown & Co., 1935.
Webb, Eugene J., *et al. Unobtrusive Measures*. Chicago: Rand McNally, 1966.
Westin, Alan F. (ed.). *An Autobiography of the Supreme Court*. New York: Macmillan Co., 1963.
———— (ed.). *The Supreme Court: Views from Inside*. New York: W. W. Norton & Co., 1961.
Wright, Charles R. *Mass Communication: A Sociological Perspective*. New York: Random House, 1959.
Young, Roland (ed.). *Approaches to the Study of Politics*. Evanston: Northwestern University Press, 1958.

C. Periodicals and Articles

"A Visit with Justice Brennan." *Look*, Dec. 18, 1962: 127–37.
Bagdikian, Ben H. "The American Newspaper Is Neither Record, Mirror, Journal, Ledger, Bulletin, Telegram, Examiner, Register, Chronicle, Gazette, Observer, Monitor, Transcript Nor Herald of the Day's Events." *Esquire*, March, 1967: 124–30, 138–46.
Bauer, Raymond A. "The Communicator and the Audience." *Journal of Conflict Resolution*, 2 (1958): 67–77.
Breed, Warren. "Newspaper 'Opinion Leaders' and the Processes of Standardization." *Journalism Quarterly*, 32 (1955): 227–84.
Brennan, William J., Jr. "Education and the Bill of Rights." *University of Pennsylvania Law Review*, 113 (1964): 219–26.
————. "Inside View of the High Court." *New York Times Magazine*, Oct. 6, 1963: 35, 100–103.
————"Law and the Social Sciences." *Vital Speeches*, Dec. 15, 1957: 143–46.
Brown, Robert U. "Shop Talk at Thirty." *Editor & Publisher*, May 12, 1956: 90.
Brucker, Herbert. "Mass Man and Mass Media." *Saturday Review*, May 29, 1965: 14–16, 44.

Bullen, Dana, "What the Supreme Court Says and What It Means." *Washington Evening Star*, Nov. 7, 1965.

Burton, Harold H. "Unsung Services of the Supreme Court of the United States." *Fordham Law Review*, 24 (1955): 169–77.

Carroll, Wallace. "Essence, Not Angle." *Columbia Journalism Review*, Summer, 1965: 4–6.

Carter, Roy E., Jr. "Newspaper 'Gatekeepers' and the Sources of News." *Public Opinion Quarterly*, 22 (1958): 133–44.

_____. "The Press and Public School Superintendents in California." *Journalism Quarterly*, 31 (1954): 175–85.

_____. "The Press, the Physician and the Public Health Officer." *American Journal of Public Health*, 49 (April, 1959): 465–72.

Charnley, Mitchell V. "Preliminary Notes on a Study of Newspaper Accuracy." *Journalism Quarterly*, 13 (1936): 394–401.

Chicago Tribune, "Highest Court Also Steeped in Tradition," Feb. 26, 1967.

Cohen, William. "Justice Douglas: A Law Clerk's View." *University of Chicago Law Review*, 26 (1958–59): 6–8.

Cranberg, Gilbert. "The Court and Its Public: Warren's View." *Des Moines Register*, Oct. 16, 1966.

_____. "What Did the Supreme Court Say?" *Saturday Review*, April 8, 1967: 90–92.

Dahl, Robert A. "Decision-Making in a Democracy: The Supreme Court as a National Policy-Maker." *Journal of Public Law*, 6 (1957): 279–95.

Deutsch, Karl W. "On Communication Models in the Social Sciences." *Public Opinion Quarterly*, 16 (1952): 356–80.

Deutschmann, Paul J., and Danielson, Wayne A. "Diffusion of Knowledge of the Major News Story." *Journalism Quarterly*, 37 (1960), 345–55.

Dirksen, Everett M. "The Supreme Court Is Defying the People." *Saturday Evening Post*, Sept. 12, 1964: 10.

Douglas, William O. "On Misconception of the Judicial Function and the Responsibilities of the Bar." *Columbia Law Review*, 59 (1959): 227–33.

_____. "Stare Decisis." *Record of the Association of the Bar of the City of New York*, 4 (1949): 152–79.

_____. "The Supreme Court and Its Case Load." *Cornell Law Quarterly*, 45 (1959–60): 401–14.

Finley, Robert C. "Who Is on Trial—The Police? The Courts? Or the Criminally Accused?" *Journal of Criminal Law and Police Science*, 57 (1966): 379–403.

Fischer, John. "The Editor's Trade." *Harper's*, July, 1965: 16–24.

Fontaine, Andre. "The Mass Media—A Need for Greatness." *The Annals*, 371 (May, 1967): 72–84.

Frank, John P. "The Top U.S. Commercial Court." *Fortune*, January, 1951: 92–96, 108–11.

Frankfurter, Felix. "The Job of a Supreme Court Justice." *New York Times Magazine*, Nov. 28, 1954: 14.

————. "The Supreme Court in the Mirror of Justices." *University of Pennsylvania Law Review*, 105 (1956–57): pp. 781–96.

Freedman, Max. "Worst Reported Institution." *Nieman Reports*, April, 1956: 2.

Freund, Paul A. "New Vistas in Constitutional Law." *University of Pennsylvania Law Review*, 112 (1963–64): 631–46.

————. "The Supreme Court Crisis." *New York State Bar Bulletin*, 30–31 (1959): 66–80.

————. "The Supreme Court Under Attack." *University of Pittsburgh Law Review*, 25 (1963–64): 1–7.

Gieber, Walter, "Across the Desk: A Study of 16 Telegraph Editors." *Journalism Quarterly*, 33 (1956): 423–32.

Glick, Edward M. "Press-Government Relationships: State and H-E-W Departments." *Journalism Quarterly*, 43 (1966): 49–56, 66.

Goldberg, Arthur J. "The Court Sits—In the Center of the Storm." *New York Times Magazine*, Nov. 8, 1964: 30, 75–78.

Graham, Fred P. "The Many-Sided Justice Fortas." *New York Times Magazine*, June 4, 1967: 26–27, 86–94.

Grey, David L. "Decision-Making by a Reporter Under Deadline Pressure." *Journalism Quarterly*, 43 (1966): 419–28.

————. "Interviewing at the Court." *Public Opinion Quarterly*, 31 (Summer, 1967): 285–89.

————. "Supreme Court Headlines: Accuracy Vs. Precision." *Columbia Journalism Review*, Summer, 1966: 26–29.

————. "Use of Ideal Types in Newsman Studies." *Journalism Quarterly*, 44 (Spring, 1967). 13–16.

Hachten, William A. "Journalism and the Prayer Decision." *Columbia Journalism Review*, Fall, 1962: 4–9; Winter, 1963: 54.

Harlan, John M. "Notes." *American Law Review*, 30 (1896): 903–5.

Harlan, John M. "What Part Does the Oral Argument Play in the Conduct of an Appeal?" *Cornell Law Quarterly*, 41 (1955–56); 6–11.

Harper, Fowler V., and Etherington, Edwin D. "Lobbyists Before the Court." *University of Pennsylvania Law Review*, 101 (1952–53): 1172–77.

Havemann, Ernest. "Storm Center of Justice." *Life*, May 22, 1964: 108–24.

Healy, Paul F. "Backstage at the Supreme Court." *Saturday Evening Post*, Jan. 2, 1960: 22–23, 49–55.

Huston, Luther A. "How the Supreme Court Reaches a Decision." *New York Times Magazine*, May 24, 1953: 11, 59–62.

Hyde, Laurance M. "Appellate Court Decisions." *American Bar Association Journal*, 28 (1942): 808–12.

Hyman, Herbert H., and Sheatsley, Paul B. "Some Reasons Why Information Campaigns Fail." *Public Opinion Quarterly*, 11 (1947): 412–23.

Jackson, Robert H. "The Law Is a Rule for Men to Live By." *Vital Speeches,* Aug. 15, 1943: 664–67.

Johnson, Earl. "Symposium: Trends Ahead in Public Affairs Reporting." *Journalism Quarterly,* 40 (1963): 441–48.

"Judicial Performance in the Fifth Circuit." *Yale Law Journal,* 73 (1963): 90–133.

Katz, Elihu, "The Two-Step Flow of Communication: An Up-To-Date Report on an Hypothesis." *Public Opinion Quarterly,* 21 (1957): 61–78.

Kaufman, Irving R. "The Supreme Court and Its Critics." *Atlantic,* December, 1963: 47–53.

Kessel, John H. "Public Perceptions of the Supreme Court." *Midwest Journal of Political Science,* 10 (1966): 167–91.

Klapper, Joseph T. "Mass Communication Research: An Old Road Resurveyed." *Public Opinion Quarterly,* 27 (1963): 515–27.

Kurland, Philip B. "On Misunderstanding the Supreme Court." *Law School Record,* 9 (1960): 13, 31–32.

_____. "The Supreme Court and Its Judicial Critics." *Utah Law Review,* 6 (1959): 457–66.

Leflar, Robert A. "Some Observations Concerning Judicial Opinions." *Columbia Law Review,* 61 (1961): 810–20.

_____. "The Task of the Appellate Court." *Notre Dame Lawyer,* 33 (1958): 548–72.

Leggett, Glenn. "Judicial Writing: An Observation by a Teacher of Writing." *Law Library Journal,* 58 (May, 1965): 114–20.

Lerner, Max. "Constitution and Court as Symbols." *Yale Law Journal,* 46 (1936–37): 1290–1319.

"Letters to the Communications Editor." *Saturday Review,* May 13, 1967: 82.

Levy, Leonard W. "School Prayers and the Founding Fathers." *Commentary,* 34 (1962): 225–30.

Lewis, Anthony. "High Drama in the High Court." *New York Times Magazine,* Oct. 26, 1958: 10, 19–20.

_____. "Historic Change in the Supreme Court." *New York Times Magazine,* June 17, 1962: 7, 36–39.

_____. "How the Supreme Court Reaches Decisions." *New York Times Magazine,* Dec. 1, 1957: 51–54.

_____. "Problems of a Washington Correspondent." *Connecticut Bar Journal,* 33 (1959): 363–71.

_____. "The Changing Role of the Supreme Court of the U.S.A." *New York State Bar Journal,* 33–34 (1961–62): 416–27.

_____. "The Court and Its Critics." *Minnesota Law Review,* 45 (1960–61): 305–32.

_____. "The Justices' Supreme Job." *New York Times Magazine,* June 11, 1961: 31–38.

————. "What Quality for the Court?" *New York Times Magazine*, Oct 6, 1957: 17, 100–102.

Lieberman, J. Ben, and Kimball, Penn T. "Educating Communicators of Specialized Subjects." *Journalism Quarterly*, 38 (1961): 527–34.

Liebes, B. H. "Decision-Making by Telegraph Editors—AP or UPI?" *Journalism Quarterly*, 43 (1966): 434–42.

Llewellyn, K. N. "The Bar Specializes—With What Results?" *The Annals*, 167 (1933): 177–92.

Loevinger, Lee. "Jurimetrics, the Next Step Forward." *Minnesota Law Review*, 33 (1948–49): 455–93.

Magruder, Calvert. "The Trials and Tribulations of an Intermediate Appellate Court." *Cornell Law Quarterly*, 44 (1958–59): 1–13.

Mason, Alpheus T. "Myth and Reality in Supreme Court Decisions." *Virginia Law Review*, 48 (1962): 1385–1406.

————. "The Supreme Court Under Fire Again," *Reporter*, Sept. 24, 1964: 45–48.

McNeil, Neil V. "The Washington Correspondents: Why Do Some 'Drop Out'?" *Journalism Quarterly*, 43 (1966): 257–63.

Milbrath, Lester W. "Lobbying as a Communication Process." *Public Opinion Quarterly*, 24 (1960): 33–53.

Murphy, Walter F. "Marshaling the Court: Leadership, Bargaining, and the Judicial Process." *University of Chicago Law Review*, 29 (1961–62): 640–72.

Nagel, Stuart S. "Law and the Social Sciences: What Can Social Science Contribute?" *American Bar Association Journal*, April, 1965: 356–58.

————, and Erikson, Robert. "Editorial Reactions to Supreme Court Decisions on Church and State." *Public Opinion Quarterly*, 30 (1966–67): 647–55.

National Council for the Social Studies. *Verdict*. Pilot Issue, 1963 (distributed as *Judgment in Social Education*, October, 1965: 361–71).

Newland, Chester A. "Press Coverage of the United States Supreme Court." *Western Political Quarterly*, 17 (1964): 15–36.

Nolan, John E., Jr. "Supreme Court v. A.B.A." *Commonweal*, May 15, 1959: 179–81.

"Passing Comment, Views of the Editors." *Columbia Journalism Review*, Fall, 1962: 2–3.

Patric, Gordon. "The Impact of a Court Decision: Aftermath of the McCollum Case." *Journal of Public Law*, 6 (1957): 455–64.

Pool, Ithiel de Sola, and Shulman, Irwin. "Newsmen's Fantasies, Audiences, and Newswriting." *Public Opinion Quarterly*, 23 (1959): 145–58.

Pusey, Merlo J. "Struggle Inside the Supreme Court." *Saturday Evening Post*, Oct. 6, 1962: 22–27.

Raskin, A. H. "What's Wrong with American Newspapers?" *New York Times Magazine*, June 11, 1967: 28–29, 77–84.

Rivers, Caryl. "Lawyer Prefers Reporting to Arguing of Big Issues." *Editor & Publisher*, Aug. 8, 1964: 42.

Rodell, Fred. "The 'Warren Court' Stands Its Ground." *New York Times Magazine*, Sept. 27, 1964: 23, 120–21.

Rosten, Leo. "The Myths By Which We Live." *Vital Speeches*, April 15, 1965: 410–14.

Schramm, Wilbur. "Information Theory and Mass Communication." *Journalism Quarterly*, 32 (1955): 131–46.

Schwartz, Bernard. "Is Criticism of the High Court Valid?" *New York Times Magazine*, Aug. 25, 1957: 14, 18–22.

Stedman, Murray S., Jr. "Pressure Groups and the American Tradition." *The Annals*, 319 (September, 1958): 123–29.

Stone, Harlan F. "The Public Influence of the Bar." *Harvard Law Review*, 48 (1934-35): 1–14.

Swinehart, James W., and McLeod, Jack M. "News About Science: Channels, Audiences, and Effects." *Public Opinion Quarterly*, 24 (1960): 583–89.

Tannenbaum, Percy H. "The Effect of Headlines on the Interpretation of News Stories," *Journalism Quarterly*, 30 (1953): 189–97.

Tarleton, Raymond J. "Accuracy and Comprehension in Science News Writing." *Journalism Quarterly*, 30 (1953): 69–71.

Vose, Clement E. "Litigation as a Form of Pressure Group Activity." *The Annals*, 319 (1958): 20–31.

Webb, Eugene J., and Salancik, Jerry R. "Notes on the Sociology of Knowledge." *Journalism Quarterly*, 42 (1965): 591–96.

Westin, Alan F. "The Business of the Court." *New York Times Book Review*, March 7, 1965: 3, 30–31.

"What's Wrong with the Press?" *Newsweek*, Nov. 29, 1965, 55–60.

Whittaker, Charles E. "A Confusion of Tongues." *American Bar Association Journal*, 51 (January, 1965): 27–32.

White, David M. "The 'Gatekeeper': A Case Study in the Selection of News." *Journalism Quarterly*, 27 (1950): 283–90.

Wiggins, J. R. "The Power and Responsibility of the Press." *Journalism Quarterly*, 37 (1960): 29–34.

Wright, Charles R. "Functional Analysis of Mass Communication." *Public Opinion Quarterly*, 24 (1960): 605–20.

Wright, J. Skelly. "A Judge's View: The News Media and Criminal Justice." *American Bar Association Journal*, 50 (December, 1964): 1125–29.

————. "The Role of the Courts: Conscience of a Sovereign People." *Reporter*, Sept. 26, 1963: 27–30.

D. Pamphlets, News Releases, and Other Documents

American Institute of Public Opinion. News Service releases: June 23, 1961; May 18, 1962; July 26, 1963; and Aug. 17, 1964.

Association of American Law Schools. *Proceedings, Part I, Reports of Committees,* 1964 and 1966 annual meetings and draft report for 1966–67 program, September, 1967.

Association of American Law Schools. *Program and Reports of Committees,* 1963 annual meeting.

Brennan, William J., Jr., "Teaching the Bill of Rights." New York: Anti-Defamation League of B'nai B'rith, 1963.

CBS Reports. "Storm Over the Supreme Court," Parts I, II, and III, Feb. 20, March 13, and June 19, 1963; and "Gideon's Trumpet: The Poor Man and the Law," Oct. 7, 1964.

Judicial Proceedings of the Judicial Conference, Sept. 30, 1938, on the Administrative Office Bill, pp. 174–92 (extract, p. 13).

Minnesota Poll, News release, *Minneapolis Sunday Tribune,* Aug. 12, 1962, and June 28, 1964.

Roper, Elmo, & Associates. News release, Oct. 19–20, 1957.

The AP Log, June 13–19, 1957.

The Docket Sheet (U.S. Supreme Court), April, 1965.

U.P. Reporter, May 3, 1956.

U.P.I. Reporter, Jan. 25, 1962.

U.S. House of Representatives. Hearings Before the Committee on the Judiciary, Part II, May 15, 1964.

Young Lawyers Committee, Federal Bar Association. *These Unalienable Rights.* Washington: Foundation of the Federal Bar Association, 1965.

E. Speeches and Other Unpublished Sources

Brennan, William J., Jr., Address, Maxwell Air Force Base, Alabama, Sept. 9, 1963.

————. Address, "Some Aspects of Federalism," Conference of Chief Justices, New York City, Aug. 7, 1964.

————. Address, "The Role of the Court—the Challenge of the Future," Edward Douglass White Lecture Series, Georgetown University Law Center, Washington, D.C., March 16, 1965.

Bullen, Dana. Address, "The Supreme Court and the Public," Vanderbilt University, Nashville, Tenn., Dec. 1, 1964.

Carroll, Wallace. Address, "The Substance, Not the Shadow," Seventh Pulitzer Memorial Lecture, Columbia University Graduate School of Journalism, New York City, May 21, 1965.

Clark, Tom C. Address, "God, Prayer and the Rights of Man," Churchman's Association, Larchmont Avenue Church, Larchmont, N.Y., Sept. 23, 1962.

Clayton, James E. Address, "News from the Supreme Court and the Justice Department," American University, Washington, D.C., May 4, 1965.

_____. Address, "The Supreme Court and Public Opinion," Edward Douglass White Lecture Series, Georgetown University Law Center, Washington, D.C., Nov. 18, 1964.

Grey, David L. Unpublished paper, "Press Coverage of the Minnesota Supreme Court," University of Minnesota School of Journalism, Minneapolis, revised version, August, 1963.

_____. Unpublished Ph.D. dissertation, "Public Communication of U.S. Appellate Court Decisions," University of Minnesota, Minneapolis, March, 1966.

Harlan, John M. Address, at dedication of New York University Law School Building, New York City, Sept. 21, 1962.

_____. Address, "Some Fiftieth Anniversary Remarks," New York County Lawyers' Association, Nov. 25, 1958.

Kaufman, Irving R. Address, "The Press, the Courts, and the Law Schools: Toward Justice and an Informed Public," Tulane Law Review Association, New Orleans, April 29, 1965.

_____. Address, seminar for new U.S. district judges, Denver, Colo., July 2, 1965.

Martin, Ann Ray. Unpublished paper, "Press Coverage of the United States Supreme Court," Washington Semester Program, American University, Washington, D.C., January, 1962.

Rivers, William L. Unpublished Ph.D. dissertation, "The Washington Correspondents and Government Information," American University, Washington, D.C., 1960.

Wheeler, Russell. "Press Coverage of the U.S. Supreme Court: How the Criminal Procedure Revolution from Mapp to Miranda was Reported in the Chicago Press." First draft of unpublished Master's thesis, University of Chicago, October, 1967 (final version, 1968).

Index

190